THE UNIVERSITY OF
WINCHESTER

Martial Rose Library
Tel: 01962 827306

06/11/14

To be returned on or before the day marked above, subject to recall.

For
Meurig Llwyd Williams

Table Manners

*Liturgical Leadership for the
Mission of the Church*

Simon Reynolds

scm press

© Simon Reynolds 2014

Published in 2014 by SCM Press
Editorial office
3rd Floor
Invicta House
108-114 Golden Lane
London
EC1Y 0TG

SCM Press is an imprint of Hymns Ancient & Modern Ltd
(a registered charity).
13A Hellesdon Park Road, Norwich NR6 5DR, UK

www.scmpress.co.uk

Illustrations by Gary Collins, absence-Presence.co.uk

British Library Cataloguing in Publication data

A catalogue record for this book is available from the British Library.

978 0 334 04528 1

Typeset by Manila Typesetting Company
Printed and bound by
Ashford Colour Press Ltd.

Contents

Acknowledgements

Without the critical encouragement of many people, this book would never have seen the light of day. Natalie Watson of SCM Press first invited me to put some initial ideas down on paper and has not only been untiring in her support throughout the subsequent writing, but infinitely patient when agreed deadlines slipped as I moved to a new parish. Bridget Nichols has long been a source of good sense and sound judgement on all things liturgical (and much more besides). I am grateful for her perceptive and sympathetic insights along the way. I only felt able to begin writing in the first place because of the generous support and encouragement of my former bishop, Stephen Platten, who exemplifies all that is best in the Anglican scholar–pastor. This is no less true of two other bishops, Stephen Oliver and Geoffrey Rowell, who generously gave their time to read the first draft of the typescript and make crucial observations.

My own formation as a priest (and liturgical president) would have been much less than it is without the companionship of Alex Hughes, Matthew Jones, Peter Waddell and Justin White, who have been delightful fellow pilgrims on the journey we began together at Westcott House, Cambridge. I am grateful, too, for the pattern and example of Alan White as I prepared for my ordination to the priesthood – and in the years beyond. Several friends, colleagues and former teachers have generously offered their insights and observations at different stages of the writing, in particular Matthew Bullimore, Julie Gittoes, Janet Henderson, Geraint Lewis, Claire Robson and Angela Tilby. Colleagues from the Diocese of Wakefield offered invaluable feedback at our triennial clergy conference in 2012; as did the clergy of the Diocese of Leicester at their 2013 clergy conference.

Malcolm Archer, Stephen Cleobury, Simon Lindley, John Scott, Huw Williams, Mark Williams and Tom Winpenny deserve much more than passing mention for the many ways in which their musical vision and creativity has enriched the liturgy – for me and for countless others – in places where I have been privileged to lead worship.

Much of the writing of this book had to be fitted around the demands and delights of parish life. I am grateful to Jean Daykin for shouldering additional burdens in the parishes of Cawthorne and Darton, which enabled me to create space for writing in the early stages. Stella Butler and her colleagues in the Brotherton Library at the University of Leeds provided me with access to sources, as well as the space to think, read and write away from the usual distractions of a priest's study.

It will be obvious that the ideas of many others have significantly influenced the shape and argument of this book. I am only too glad to acknowledge them in the text, the bibliography and footnotes. Any consequent deficiencies are entirely my responsibility.

Simon Reynolds
Farnham
Feast of Gregory the Great
3 September 2013

Introduction

Week after week I was moved by the pitiableness of the bare linoleum-floored sacristy which no flowers could cheer or soften, by the terrible singing I so loved, by the fatigued Bible readings, the lagging emptiness and dilution of the liturgy, the horrifying vacuity of the sermon, and by the fog of dreary senselessness pervading the whole, which existed alongside, and probably caused, the wonder of the fact that we came; we returned; we showed up; week after week, we went through it. (Dillard, 1982, p. 29)

Is there a liturgical crisis in the Church of England? (Williams, in Papadopulos, 2011, p. 1)

In Great Britain, less than 10 per cent of the population attends a Christian place of worship once a week; and just under two per cent of the population attend worship in an Anglican Church.

- What is it that attracts people to Christian worship in a predominantly secular, multi-cultural society?
- What do they experience in church – and what expectations do they bring with them?
- What is it about their worshipping experience which encourages them to return?
- Is there an encounter with the holy, and is the worshipping environment having a transformative impact?
- Do worshippers emerge from liturgical celebration into the market place of competing values feeling delighted and inspired or bored and despairing?

- Did the person who presided at worship convey a sense of the immediacy and reality of God through the use of voice and gestures and by appropriate use of language, space, music and symbols?

I believe these are timely questions for many Christian churches and for the Church of England in particular. The past decade has witnessed an unprecedented proliferation of new liturgical texts, which is the culmination of over 50 years of continuous liturgical revision in our Church. The scope of our authorized liturgy is now richer than in any previous period since the publication of the first Book of Common Prayer in 1549. Yet, there is a growing anxiety about the quality of worship being offered in the Church of England, particularly in what might be characterized as 'ordinary' parish churches. Much of this (disquietingly) seems to have become focused on the competence of those who preside at worship – especially in relation to their formation and training before and after ordination.

This anxiety has been expressed with characteristic clarity by the former Archbishop of Canterbury, Rowan Williams:

Part of my concern about the situation with liturgy in our Church is not so much with the disappearance of this or that text from education and practice or with the shift in style, but with a fairly pervasive failure to realize that people do need to be educated in liturgical behaviour. By which of course I do not mean what angle to hold your thumbs . . . I mean liturgical behaviour: using your body significantly. A great many people emerge from our training institutions with very little sense of what that might mean, or of how the use of the celebrant's body enables or disables the whole community's worship. But no theological student is going to grasp that without some theology to underpin it.

(Williams, in Papadopulos, 2011, p. 12)

Does it Matter?

Traditionally, Anglican identity has been shaped by the way we worship. It has been shaped by the theology which underpins our liturgical rites and by the language and gestures used to articulate this theology. It has also been shaped by the history and culture in which these rites have developed and by the way they are 'presented' today. Of course, there have been developments and influences over recent decades which have eroded this traditional understanding of the Anglican character, not least from those whose faith and ecclesial identity is being formed in isolation from our liturgical rites (whether catholic or reformed). Nonetheless, I hope that, by restating this foundational trait, as well as emphasizing the interdependence of our dogmatic stance and the words and actions of our worship, it will become clear that the quality of worship, and the quality of liturgical presidency in particular, matters precisely because liturgy forms the bedrock of Anglican mission.

My own repeated experience is that presiding at the liturgy is the most demanding, privileged and exhausting thing I do. It is the overarching action which enables me to embody the vocation I have embraced as a priest. It reinforces everything else I am called to do as preacher, pastor, mission-enabler, administrator, teacher, encourager and builder of community. Wherever I have had the privilege of presiding at worship, it has become self-evident that the quality of worship – its spatial setting, its verbal, musical and symbolic content and the overall quality of presidency – can be a crucial dimension in enabling seekers and enquirers to gain a foothold in the life of the Church. It has helped them to feel they can discover a place to belong alongside more established worshippers and explore more thoroughly the contours of Christian life and faith. In my present context, I have found that, by our investing a degree of energy in attempting to provide imaginative and engaging worship, we are better equipped to do mission as a 'parish-shaped' church.[1]

It would be reasonable to assume, therefore, that the theology, history and practice of liturgy is given a significant (if not central) place in the formation of our clergy, in the priorities we set for mission (locally and nationally) and in the underpinning of pastoral practice. We should take it for granted that presiding at the liturgy (and more specifically at the Eucharist) should be at the heart of formation for presbyteral ministry, precisely because what is discovered, confronted, learned and embodied in the act of presiding underpins, informs and nourishes every other aspect of ministry exercised by the ordained. If those who preside at the Eucharist embody what the whole church is called to be as a community of mission, they should be properly equipped to demonstrate what the Church has to offer those who are seeking and enquiring. As Andrew Walker has identified:

> Liturgy, as divine drama, tells again the old, old story . . . [it] demands words and images of wisdom and power, theologically significant body language, lights, colours, smells and food. If we are asking contemporary culture to 'come and see', we must have something to show them as well as something to say. (1996, p. 99)

Challenges and Opportunities

The challenge to which this book seeks to respond is a question posed by Rowan Williams, just over a decade after the publication of the first stream of *Common Worship*, the most recent liturgical texts in the Church of England: 'Is there a liturgical crisis in the Church of England?' (Williams, in Papadopulos, 2011, p. 1). This book is written from the conviction that, if this crisis

---

1 This expression was first coined by Graham James, see 'Mission; and the Parish-Shaped Church', *Theology*, 109:847, 2006.

is real, it presents the Church with significant challenges and opportunities: not simply in the narrow (and currently marginalized) arena of liturgical study and practice; but in rethinking the emphases of ministerial formation, in taking seriously the public potential of liturgy in a cultural climate of antagonism towards the narratives and symbols of faith, as well as the liturgy's capacity to form, re-form and define the character of the Church and to draw others into its pattern of life and belief.

My starting point is to examine how the Church of England's current policy towards liturgical formation in ministry training may be found wanting, as well as identifying the cultural momentum which has informed and accompanied the renewal of the liturgy in recent decades, to ask how these factors might inform a more imaginative re-appraisal of this currently marginalized component in ministry training.

I move on to explore some of the issues which might assist a search for the origins and development of Christian worship and, more significantly, how these origins might inform a renewal of contemporary practice. Although I assume a rudimentary familiarity with the basics of Christian liturgical origins by readers, my concern here is not so much to repeat what others have already identified. Rather, I hope to pinpoint some examples of more recent scholarship which might challenge previously long-held assumptions, as well as suggesting how recent developments in historical understanding could helpfully clarify a renewed understanding of what a liturgical president is called to embody at the celebration of the Eucharist in a contemporary context.

Chapters 3–5 examine some of the practical dimensions which inform – and challenge – presidential practice and styles, by addressing spoken and written language, body language, architectural space, symbolism and colour, within the framework of the historic, cultural, philosophical and theological climate which has shaped contemporary perceptions and expectations.

Chapter 6 offers some suggestions for cultivating pastoral, theological and liturgical habits which might become part of a president's ministry and spirituality, highlighting practices, disciplines, skills and attitudes which may enable presidents (and the worshipping communities they lead) to be enlarged, enriched and equipped by the experience of worship.

I write from the experience of working not only in a cathedral, with all the professional and financial resources that are de rigeur; but also in what might be described as 'ordinary' parish churches. Until very recently, my ministry was based in South Yorkshire and focused on former mining communities with modest financial means, architectural constraints, an often smaller pool of creative talent, sometimes lower expectations and infinitely less 'pulling power' than our iconic centres of excellence. I hope this experience will root the discussion in the earthed realities in which many readers will find themselves worshipping and ministering. I also hope it will demonstrate why I am posing challenges which may question elements of existing practice and encourage the discovery of previously unconsidered possibilities.

Above all, my hope is that those who are given the awesome privilege and responsibility of presiding at the Church's defining act of worship will recognize the fundamental importance of being well formed (and informed) in the tradition into which they are being invited to participate. It is one means of discovering how intelligent and sensitive liturgical presidents can become vital and necessary enablers of mission, whose primary task it is to meet what Philip Larkin has described as 'the hunger to be more serious' (Larkin, 'Church-Going', 2003).

Enchantment or Entertainment? The Challenge and Potential of the Contemporary Liturgical Culture

We *make* ritual, even inherited and prescribed ritual, because we bring to it a network of association and intention which shapes its meaning for us . . . in every celebration of the liturgy there is always more going on than the words, rubrics or intentions of the celebrant or the liturgists explicitly envisage. (Duffy, 1996, p. 883)

When I preside at the Eucharist, I do so as an embodied and inter-related person. I 'go to the altar' carrying a complex weight of baggage – and expectation – which is personal, social, ecclesial, historical and theological. How I preside has been shaped by the impetus and influence of an evolving tradition, by my own reflection on the history and practice of Christian worship, by the theology which has informed that historical momentum and by the hopes and expectations of those I will lead in the celebration of the Eucharist. To preside at the Eucharist is to be ineradicably related to other people, other times, other insights and other influences which are not of my own making. I have discovered that this calls for both heightened sensitivity and a large degree of realism in recognizing that much of what I say, sing or do in the act of presiding belongs not to me, but to others. This is where a good dollop of humility comes in handy because I have to acknowledge that it will not always be 'easy' or 'accessible'. The linguistic, theological, musical, symbolic and spatial dimension I am called to embody when I preside will not always be immediately understood by those I am called to lead in worship.

Nonetheless, if I have some measure of confidence in the task entrusted to me and a reasonably firm sense of where I fit into the unfolding story of the development of Christian worship, as well as possessing a basic grasp of the theological tradition which continues to shape my exercise of this ministry, I stand a better chance of drawing those for whom the unlikeness of the liturgy may be as fascinating as it is unexplained into the mysteries which nourish and sustain all Christians.

However, I detect that the 'liturgical crisis', which I highlighted in the Introduction and which I suggest the Church is currently experiencing, is more often than not located in a lack of confidence – even competence – on the part of those who are called to preside at the Eucharist. As David Stancliffe has tersely (but accurately) diagnosed:

> I mind a lot about worship, and wonder at the quality of what is offered in many places in this most important area of the Church's life. In an age when the standards of public performance are so high, how do worshippers manage to keep on going to church faithfully when the way worship is prepared and offered is often so dire; when it is frequently confused with entertainment, and when it is led by those who apparently have no idea what they are doing or professional competence in doing it? (2003, p. xiii)

A Culture of Competence?

As the principal architect of *Common Worship*, Stancliffe's vision of the shape and content of the Church's liturgy impacts directly on the lives of countless worshippers and on those who are called to preside at it. He clearly identifies that, in a context of mission, those who come to worship do so with heightened expectations. This is especially true of those whose experience of the Church's worship is occasional or rare. The Church ministers in a consumerist culture, where worship is often just another disposable commodity; and worshippers (whether regular or infrequent), whose expectations have been shaped by the social and cultural expectations of the present moment, can be disappointed and diminished by what they experience in church – despite the unprecedented liturgical creativity of the past half century. Those whose only contact with the liturgical life of the Church is through public broadcasting networks, for example, will be exposed to consistently high standards of music, preaching, use of architectural space and slick treatment of the visual and aural.

Those of us who work in typical parochial situations cannot ignore the capacity of the media to shape the expectations of those who worship in our churches – whether regularly or rarely. Account needs to be taken of the way the BBC, for example, has largely moved away from broadcasting typically 'parochial' acts of worship on radio and television, but is concentrating instead on cathedrals and other centres of excellence. The weekly Sunday prime-time hymn-singing BBC programme *Songs of Praise* has not only become more of an entertainment experience; it is also dominated by professional musicians (choirs, orchestras, organists as well as personalities from the world of popular music) and employs sophisticated lighting and camera techniques to such an extent that it is no longer said to depict worship in most parish churches. I recognize that such comparisons can be debilitating, especially to those liturgical presidents who recognize the need to 'raise the bar' but who lack the financial, architectural and human resources to emulate the media ideals. Nonetheless, the fact that this expectation is 'out there' beyond the formal worshipping life of the Church holds up to presidents and worshippers alike a challenge: not so much to strive for slick technology, but more to aspire to the BBC's absolute focus on professionalism, attention to detail and confidence in their broadcasting tradition.

Echoing David Stancliffe's insights, Peter Moger, as the Church of England's National Worship Development Officer

(2005–9), was instrumental in developing and implementing a programme of liturgical formation, *Transforming Worship*. Broadly aimed at encouraging practitioners and worshipping communities to examine how, having received new texts, their worship might contribute to nurture and growth, it also posed some challenging theological and missiological questions. Such a promising programme appears to have been limited in its overall impact, largely because it was never absorbed in any significant way into programmes of training for ordained ministry. With hindsight, it has also highlighted the degree to which the *Common Worship* project had concentrated on producing texts before the more basic task of attempting to change the worshipping culture in which those texts would be used. Shortly after moving from this post (which was then reduced to half-time for his successor), Moger could see that

> [w]ould-be worship leaders (lay and ordained) are in need of a solid grounding in the liturgical principles of structure and flow, based on an understanding of worship as a *transformative* process [my italics]. There is greater need for a clear understanding of the times and seasons of the Christian year, and of the interplay of Scripture, liturgy and theology . . . Ministers need to be equipped to make intelligent choices, to develop the practice of thinking liturgically and, in a 'mixed-economy' church . . . [t]he challenge stretches across both periods of Initial Ministerial Education: 1–3 (the years of training at college, or on a course or scheme) and 4–7 (the years immediately following ordination or licensing), and beyond. (Moger, in Papadopulos, 2011, pp. 138–9)

Stancliffe and Moger not only identify the effects of the paucity of liturgical formation for those who are given the authority to preside at the Church of England's worship, they also hint at the low expectations the Church currently has of its ordained ministers when it comes to the skills and sensitivities needed to preside well at the liturgy.

Ecumenical Perspectives

For Roman Catholics, the art of liturgical presidency is foundational to the formation of priests, and the assumption underpinning ordination training is that

> the study and practice of the sacred liturgy is to be ranked among the compulsory and major courses in seminaries . . . It is to be taught under its theological, historical, spiritual, pastoral, and juridical aspects . . . The strict connection between the liturgy and the doctrine of the Faith has a special importance for the correct liturgical formation of future priests . . . [those] working in the field of sacred liturgy are to investigate carefully the tradition of divine worship, particularly when they study the nature of the Church and the doctrine and discipline of the sacraments . . . (*Instructions on Liturgical Formation in Seminaries*, Sacred Congregation for Catholic Education)

Similarly, the formation of all the baptized has a foundational liturgical dimension. The Rite of Christian Initiation of Adults (RCIA) in the Roman Catholic Church is grounded in a series of liturgical celebrations, leading to baptism and admission to the sacramental life and firmly linked to the rhythm of the paschal cycle of the liturgical year (Lent, Easter and Pentecost). In a process that consciously draws on the mystagogical patterns of the Early Church and the writings of personalities such as Ambrose of Milan (d. 397) and Cyril of Jerusalem (d. 386), it understands formation not simply as a matter of teaching the Church's dogmatic and scriptural categories, but of the transformation of the whole person through participation in liturgical celebration:

> the entire [process] is ordered towards leading . . . candidates to living a true liturgical life, permeated by prayer and worship within the Body of Christ and punctuated by regular participation in the sacraments, especially the Eucharist . . .

it is vital that it be communicated that the liturgy *is* their means to achieve holiness. All knowledge of the Faith, practice of spiritual and corporal works of mercy, and obedience to the laws of the New Covenant flow from the liturgical life. (RCIA, Introduction, p. 71)

In the Methodist Church, before a person can undertake diaconal or presbyteral ministry, they are required to have first exercised a sustained ministry as a Local Preacher. The underlying assumption is that the foundation for the exercise of ministry is the embodiment of scripture, experience, tradition and reason in the liturgical arena – and, more specifically, the pulpit. The current syllabus for the training and formation of Methodist local preachers begins with the specifics of leading worship, before moving on to a consideration of scripture and doctrine. Something of this dynamic has always traditionally been present in the Free Churches' understanding of their ordained ministries and is best summarized by the Baptist scholar, Neville Clark:

> the ministry is to be defined not by its functions, not even by its gifts, but in the end by the mysterious realities it is commissioned to serve and bear . . . Word and sacrament constitute the cohesive centre of the ministerial vocation, and therefore and thereby the worship of the people of God is the unifying arena of ministerial life. (1991, p. 15)

Anglican Reticence

The Church of England, by contrast, has been generally more reticent about giving this dimension of ministerial (and more specifically priestly) formation a central place. At the time of writing, there are just 38 words (in a document of over 1,600 words) referring to the need for basic liturgical competence in the national syllabus for pre-ordination training in the Church of England. At the point of ordination, candidates should:

Be rooted in corporate worship in the traditions and practices of the Church of England, showing gifts and ability in leading public worship and preaching in ways that show understanding of and good practice in liturgy and worship. (Learning Outcome Statement for Ordained Ministry in the Church of England)[1]

Although there are basic courses in the foundations of Christian worship in colleges and on courses, which address the history and practice of liturgy, it is largely assumed that much of a priest's liturgical *formation* will take place in the title parish. In the year following ordination as a deacon, under the supervision of a training incumbent (who is similarly assumed to be sufficiently grounded in the theological, historical and practical dimensions of liturgical celebration), a recently ordained minister is supposed to be equipped to be a sensitive, competent and imaginative presider at the liturgy. Additionally, a group session (and it is rarely more than one) may be provided at diocesan level in the months leading up to a person's presbyteral ordination, which is often characterized by a concern with 'what to wear' and 'what to do with your hands'. That presiding at the liturgy might be a central feature of training for ordination or is rooted in rigorous theological reflection does not always seem apparent.

Currently, there are basic courses in the foundations of Christian worship in colleges and on courses; and there are encouraging proposals, under the Common Awards scheme for initial ministerial education, which address the history and practice of liturgy in considerably more depth than is the case at present. Significantly, the liturgical modules are weighted on an equal footing with biblical studies, doctrine and ethics, reflective and practical theology. Nonetheless, if the development of the skills and sensitivities for good presidency continues to be confined

---

1 At www.churchofengland.org/media/56877/The%20learning%20outcomes.doc.

to the title or 'home' parish, it is questionable whether any significant progress will result.

Present experience suggests that this strategy has been found wanting. There are exceptions, but the self-evident outcome is that significant numbers of those who are authorized to preside at the Church's worship are not only ill-equipped for the task, but lack clarity about what makes their ministry as a liturgical president distinctive. This can only engender a general uncertainty and lack of confidence about how informed decisions might be made, but also by what criteria good liturgical presidency might inform and inspire the growth and mission of the whole people of God.

Undergirding questions of training and formation are more fundamental issues concerned with the present-day culture of the Church, a presider's spirituality and theological character, personal, aesthetic and spatial awareness and a heightened perception of how the liturgical president 'embodies' the mysteries at the heart of the Church's proclamation of the Gospel. It may be relatively easy to name what is 'dire' about a particular act of worship; it is less easy to impart a sense of how liturgical presidents might develop an instinct for the art of presiding. Possessing the capacity to evoke transcendence, to enable worship to be a transformative experience, of cultivating a passion to lead worshippers beyond themselves to glimpse the possibility of God's otherness, is infinitely more complex and demanding.

A Culture of 'Liturgiophobia'?

I retain particularly vivid memories of being part of a panel interviewing candidates for a director of pastoral studies vacancy at a Church of England theological college, just as the Church was engaged in its most intensive period of liturgical creativity and revision. One of the candidates confidently asserted that, in the pastoral formation of ordinands, there was a need for 'ritual to be replaced by praxis'. In the questions that followed, I probed this assertion. The candidate explained that 'ritual' broadly meant the history and theology, as well as the insights, instincts and sensitivities required to preside well at the liturgy; adding that 'we do not so much need well turned-out deacons as insightful pastors'. This led me to ask how ritual and praxis could ever be considered mutually exclusive in the formation of pastors and theologians whose primary task would be to 'unfold the Scriptures, to preach the word in season and out of season, and to declare the mighty acts of God . . . to preside at the Lord's table and lead his people in worship, offering with them a spiritual sacrifice of praise and thanksgiving . . . to bless the people in God's name . . .' (*Common Worship* 'Ordination of Priests'). The candidate responded by insisting that liturgy was 'a place of safety' and that real theological and pastoral formation took place not in the college chapel (or in the orbit of the worshiping community where a recently ordained person would serve), but in other arenas such as the youth group, in ministering to the bereaved or in setting up a social outreach programme at the margins of church life. Liturgy, it was strongly implied, was merely a bolt-on to more 'authentic' modes of pastoral and theological formation.

To be fair to the candidate described in this situation, the adopted stance was merely a reflection of the climate of 'liturgiophobia' that has unquestioningly prevailed in many of our training institutions (and among some of our bishops!) for several decades. At one level, this has been an understandable reaction to an unhealthy sub-culture, which has been uncritically preoccupied with allegedly 'correct' or 'authentic' liturgical behaviour to the detriment of those aspects of training and formation which are a necessary consequence of having been immersed in the history, theology and practice of presiding at the Church's liturgy. Nonetheless, as Stanley Hauerwas has written of his wife, who is a Methodist presbyter:

> For her the ministry is not the name of a 'helping profession'. You do not need to be ordained to help people. Rather, she clearly thinks she was ordained to preside at the Eucharist. (2010, p. 214)

This insight pinpoints the degree to which there persists a residual reliance on the assumptions of figures such as Carl Rogers, whose client-centred and value-free model of pastoral counselling contributed significantly to the training for pastoral care in the twentieth century. An overdependence on this model has created an environment in which fundamental theological perspectives became marginalized by a primary emphasis on the human sciences. The work of figures such as Don Browning (1976) and Elaine Graham (1996) has been formative in challenging these assumptions. However, a distinctively Anglican approach to ministerial formation cannot ignore the liturgical implications of recognizing that

> [t]he difficulty with much of pastoral counselling today is that more time is spent in discussing the tools of counselling than in the more challenging process of developing the structures of meanings that should constitute the context for counselling. (Browning, 1976, p. 109)

Much of the inherent imbalance in pastoral care can be traced back to the various ways in which Christianity has responded to the challenges of the Reformation and the developments which followed in its wake. The liturgical dimension of this response has been identified, among others, by the Roman Catholic moral philosopher Jonathan Robinson. He asks to what extent the Church, in its desire to renew and revise the liturgy, has been overdependent on the assumptions of the Enlightenment by speaking of an 'anthropocentric liturgy' and a Church 'turned in on itself' (2005, p. 34). This is especially the case when it comes to the interdependency of liturgy and social engagement where, Robinson claims, ethical concerns have completely engulfed the Church's sacramental life or have been reduced to little more than a convenient venue for the presentation of moral values. Instead, the liturgy should constitute that 'structure of meaning' which Browning has identified and from which the Church should engage imaginatively with a fractured world:

If we take the sacraments seriously, then we have to take the importance of the visible church seriously. The Church is more than a society for the promotion of the ethics of duty; she is Christ's mystical body here on earth where the mercy of God is found in the sacraments. (2005, p. 94)

Robinson's insights are echoed by the Catholic historian, Eamon Duffy, who highlights the extent to which much liturgical revision in the twentieth century has taken place in parallel with a period of profound cultural dislocation in the West.

Genuine theological renewal became inextricably tangled with a shallow and philistine repudiation of the past which was to have consequences as disastrous in theology as they were in the fine arts, architecture and city planning. (1996, p. 882)

This suggests that the theological interpretation of the ideals of the Second Vatican Council and in particular its liturgical outworking (which also found expression across most Western Christian denominations) has come to be seen, in certain respects, as not so much radical as one-dimensional. An over-anxious concern to mirror the contemporary cultural momentum resulted in an imbalance which obscured the equally pressing need to be refreshed and renewed by the sources and origins of the tradition. How this interpretative task, particularly as it related to the liturgy, may have been uncritically pre-occupied with a selective reading of history is discussed in subsequent chapters (see especially pages 49 and 50). It is nonetheless significant that, in the period which anticipated the Second Vatican Council, Henri de Lubac was one of a number of theologians writing about the need to rediscover the roots of the tradition as the first step in reclaiming the Gospel's significance for contemporary culture. This excavation of the roots and sources of faith was termed *ressourcement*. It was to provide the foundational stratum which would facilitate a renewed articulation of the Gospel, expressed as *aggiornamento*. The necessity for both dimensions to be held in creative tension was of fundamental importance to de Lubac:

> The renewal of Christian vitality is linked at least partially to a renewed exploration of the periods and of the works where the Christian tradition is expressed with a particular intensity . . . in so far as we have allowed it to be lost, we must rediscover the *spirit* of Christianity. In order to do so we must be plunged once more into its well-springs . . . (1995, p. 72)

This theological dynamic, which invited a rigorous commitment to *ressourcement*, might potentially have led those responsible for liturgical renewal from the 1950s onwards to a realization that 'full, active and conscious participation' would not inevitably lead to a mode of worship which now appears not only reductionist, but has left several generations of worshippers isolated from the roots of a multifaceted liturgy as it has evolved through Christian history. Liturgically, *aggiornamento* not only proved to be historically selective in certain respects, it also led to an interpretative application in which the theological dimension was obscured by anthropological insights and a communitarian emphasis which feels as if it has eclipsed the fundamental purpose of worship as an encounter with the mystery and reality of God. In other words, the emphasis given to divine immanence in the midst of the worshipping community has become so pervasive that many worshippers will struggle to sense how it is held in creative tension with a belief in the divine presence transcending a particular community gathered for worship at a particular place and time.

It would be easy to caricature the outcome, with its 'horizontal' linguistic, musical, spatial and environmental impact; where cultural relevance and communitarian dynamics have become prized above the desire and longing for the transcendent and liminal. Suffice to say that what emerged, liturgically, for Protestants as well as Catholics, was mirrored in the theological, pastoral and cultural assumptions that accompanied the formation of those preparing for ordained ministry. For Anglicans in particular, a rigorous embracing of the principles which inform *ressourcement* should have unavoidably pinpointed the liturgy as the primary arena of our distinctive theological and pastoral bearing towards those we are called to serve.

Confidence or Crisis?

The ambivalence towards the significance of liturgical presidency in the formation for ministry in the Church of England has, on the whole, resulted in a complex climate of guilt, embarrassment, indifference, insecurity and even antipathy towards this foundational characteristic of ordained ministry. We have made a 'big deal' of it when, far from being self-conscious, it should be an innate and spontaneous foundation to the theological and pastoral formation of priests, deacons – and especially bishops as chief pastors and the normative ministers of word and sacrament. There is, in short, an underlying lack of confidence in the role and person of the liturgical president.

Conversations with clergy colleagues suggest that the majority of them, while acknowledging the importance of leading Sunday worship, speak of little more than 'cursory' liturgical formation prior to ordination (unless they chose to specialize in some aspect of its study). They consequently devote comparatively little time now to preparing for it, reviewing it, availing themselves of further liturgical training, or feel confident in encouraging their parochial church councils to commit financial or other resources to developing or enhancing it. And yet it is of some significance that one of the two areas of sustained growth in the Church of England over the past decade has been those places (notably cathedrals, larger city-centre churches and collegiate foundations) which invest considerable resources in promoting liturgical and musical excellence (see below, p. 21).

Patterns of Ministry Training

Until relatively recently, the underlying assumption was that training and formation for ordained ministry in the Church of England would take place in a residential (quasi-monastic) community with a stable pattern of twice-daily corporate worship, punctuated by occasional experiment and variety. My own experience on such a pathway reflected this liturgical pattern, supplemented by a significant degree of good practice and variety on the college's doorstep (whether in or out of my 'comfort zone'), providing opportunities to absorb both the essential *stabilitas* as well as innovative dimensions of the Church's (and the churches') worship. No one ever deliberately taught me *how* to preside at the Eucharist (other than facilitating the odd 'dry run' close to the time of my ordination as a priest). Instead, I absorbed it (and continue to absorb it) by a kind of 'attentive osmosis'. In such a context, it was possible to be formed, to a large degree, by almost daily exposure to consistently good practice, across the spectrum of traditions, by those who were confident in the role they embodied. This enlarged my experience of liturgical practice well beyond my 'home' church and enabled me to identify good role models from different traditions. It also meant that my experience of leading worship, whether in the college chapel or in placement situations, was not only informed by regularly observed and experienced good practice, but was subject to regular review and assessment rooted in an ongoing liturgical momentum.

Financial, demographic and ecclesiological factors have all played a part in creating a situation where just over half of those currently preparing for ordained ministry in the Church of England (2012–13) are experiencing a completely different mode of training and formation. In these situations, there is no structured and disciplined pattern of daily worship within the peer group, led by experienced and effective liturgical presidents or with sustained and constructive feedback offered to those who lead worship as students. Instead, ordinands meet for evening teaching on weekdays and, apart from placements related to their course, continue to worship in their 'home' church. A number of weekends each year, with a particular thematic focus, provide the substantial residential element of formation. However, because there is no collectively owned liturgical rhythm to 'pick up' at such occasions, worship tends to be confected to resonate with the theme under scrutiny; and the potential to experience the regular and stable pattern of the Church's foundational liturgy appears to be eclipsed by the pressure to be endlessly 'creative'. In this way, corporate worship carries the implicit burden of either unrelenting novelty or confused expectation. The potential for ordinands to 'inhabit' collectively a stable liturgical pattern, alongside any inventive or experimental worship, where a critical and reflective sensitivity to the dynamics of presiding may be cultivated, underpinned by theological rigour and sustained exposure to good practice, appears somewhat limited.

That is not to say that the residential pathway uniformly produces competent, sensitive and imaginative liturgical presidents, any more than the emphasis given to liturgical formation by our ecumenical partners has resulted in a consistently high quality of worship in Roman Catholic or Methodist churches, for example. The absence of much sustained attention to liturgical formation across the Church of England's training institutions and courses has created a climate where ordinands are encouraged – indeed, expected – to develop their critical faculties in relation to pastoral encounters and the contexts for mission and ministry (by the keeping of regular journals, for example, as well as the employment of reflective models of praxis). However, much less attention seems to be given to critical reflection on the liturgical consequences of such encounters and how liturgical presidency relates to mission and pastoral care. This is all the more surprising in the light of the sustained attention given to the interdependence of liturgy and pastoral care in significant writing over the past three decades.[2] It is not difficult to discern how, in a learning environment where

---

2 For example Green (1987), Ramshaw (1987), Willimon (1979).

outcomes and objectives have become the overriding priority, less measurable and more implicit emphases can become marginalized in the syllabus. As Robert Hovda has identified,

> [c]hurches that have been preoccupied for centuries with other aspects of their corporate lives have taken the function, office, task of presiding in liturgy for granted. Not much time has been spent defining it. Not much thought has been given to aptitude and qualifications for its exercise. It has been widely assumed that whoever is ordained must be ready, and scrutinies before ordination are rarely concerned with what will be the candidate's most prominent activity after ordination. (1986, p. 7)

Nonetheless, the foundational task of the formation of the people of God, as well as the very pastoral and missionary encounters on which candidates for ordained ministry are encouraged to reflect at such depth, have unavoidable liturgical consequences. This is most visibly the case in the sacraments and pastoral offices of baptism, marriage and funerals, as well as the regular pattern of weekly worship in a parish. These are, for the majority of parochial clergy, the primary opportunity for the Church and its worship to touch the lives of those who are largely beyond its regular worshipping life. Very often, those who are being trained and formed to preside at such significant life-events are implicitly (if not explicitly) discouraged from investing the energy and imagination required to ensure that the pastoral and theological dimension is afforded the significant and engaging linguistic, musical and symbolic expression they require. Moreover, the empathetic, intuitive qualities necessary for pastoral care are as basic to the expression of grief and joy in the liturgical arena as they are for a funeral visit, for example. It is becoming apparent, in some contexts, that the Church's liturgy is assumed to be an 'internal' activity, geared to the needs of those who worship most regularly and who have devised a pattern that works best for a particular president or worshipping community. And yet it is this propensity to regard liturgy as a largely 'domestic' matter which can be deeply undermining of the Church's missionary bearing towards its wider social and cultural setting.

Public Significance

The challenge posed by the peripheral status of liturgical formation for ministry brings into sharp focus a crucial missiological question: how *public* is the Church's ordained ministry expected to be in the future? This is especially germane when the language of 'mission' is a dominant motif in many areas of Christian formation, but is often assumed to refer to activities *other than* worship. However, the etymological root of the Greek word 'liturgy' has unavoidable public associations which are bound up with notions of community cohesion and the common good. Originally, its 'secular' use referred to public service, of individuals carrying out a task which served the needs of wider society.

Similarly, to 'preside' is to be visible – and visible beyond the internal life of the Church – in a distinctive and representative way. In a climate of ecclesial decline, with falling numbers of deployable clergy, serving a context which remains sceptical about the place of faith in public discourse, the significance and value of the Church's liturgy in enabling a distinctive theological voice to be heard in the 'secular' sphere is both compelling and obvious.

The stance of the Anglican clergy has traditionally been that of scholar–pastor, where it has been largely assumed that a priest will embody the Christian tradition through a corpus of learning (not simply 'theology' in the narrowly defined sense of what a syllabus may provide; but languages, the arts and sciences, as well as history, literature and 'popular culture') which feeds a capacity to contribute to public discourse with confidence. This is much less the case, today; and the Church's liturgy is, perhaps, the one remaining arena where a distinctive theological dimension can be heard – and experienced. The discernible tendency of the Church in decline has been to direct its energy inwards. The need for liturgical presidents who can 'speak outwardly' into the public sphere with an appropriate degree of confidence, sensitivity and thoughtfulness is becoming self-evidently urgent. Reflecting on his ministry as a parish priest, Michael Sadgrove recognizes that

> my role as celebrant extended well beyond the boundaries of the regular Sunday congregation . . . I began to see how the Church's worship 'represents' and makes conscious the unarticulated worship of creation . . . I saw how my role as a priest was to interpret the life of both community and individuals in the light of faith in God. This is one of the prime functions of liturgy. (2008, pp. 100–1)

At national and international level, a series of terrors and tragedies (the death of Princess Diana in 1997, 9/11 in New York, 7/7 in London, for example) have demonstrated that where the Church's liturgy has been undergirded by a high degree of theological rigour and pastoral sensitivity, it has not only attracted a substantial degree of positive media coverage; it has also given those beyond the regular worshipping life of the Church a stake in its language and symbols. It has touched the unspoken and unrecognized depths of human experience in a surprising and, perhaps, previously unacknowledged way.

At a local level, those whose contact with the Church is occasional or rare still seek liturgical moments which articulate their needs – whether in grief of celebration – and will be able to identify when a liturgical experience has been positive or not. It is notoriously tricky to define exactly how theological integrity, human empathy and artistic imagination mesh in such a way that people emerge from an act of worship feeling both affirmed and transformed; but most people can say when it has been embarrassing, monotonous and thoroughly uninviting.

A church in one of the parishes I previously served was the venue for the military funeral of a young Territorial Army volunteer who had been killed by an improvised explosive device while serving in Afghanistan. It demanded not only clarity about the theological assumptions which needed to underpin such an act of worship, the expectations of the deceased's regiment, his workmates at a local factory, as well as the clearly expressed wishes of his family; it also required a patient and focused attention to what the wider community was feeling about the loss of 'one of its own' – coupled to the need for vigilance about how the event might be championed by the local branch of the British National Party. There were moments where the expectations of all who had a stake in this funeral were variously challenged and affirmed, where account was taken of the representative nature of the occasion, as well as time spent addressing the very private grief of a local family who had become the unwilling and unexpected focus of public attention. Formality and informality had to be sensitively judged, as did the choice of music (not least when I found myself having to step in to direct a group of teenagers who wanted to perform a dance routine to a track by the Arctic Monkeys which, left to their own devices, could have left them – and the congregation – feeling embarrassed and diminished). At heart, the issue that faced us was the degree to which the occasion was being variously emphasized as ecclesiastical, civic, cultural and deeply personal. How well we achieved a 'satisfactory outcome' for all concerned is difficult to judge. Nonetheless, it was manifestly not an internal or churchy activity, but required a depth of insight and engagement which was self-evidently 'theology' and 'pastoral care' in the public sphere. But it was unapologetically rooted in a conviction that the liturgical dimension was fundamental.

There is, of course, nothing novel about this wider pastoral and social dimension to liturgical presidency. The first use of the term 'president' in relation to one who leads the Eucharistic celebration is found in the *Apology* of Justin Martyr (d. *c*.100). After a description of the bare bones of the Eucharistic rite (which will be familiar to most worshippers today), we are told that, after the distribution of communion is completed, those who are absent [receive] a portion . . . sent by the deacons. And they who are well to do, and willing, give what each thinks fit; and what is collected is deposited with the president, who succours the orphans and widows and those who, through sickness or any other cause, are in want, and those who are in bonds and the strangers sojourning among us, and in a word takes care of all who are in need. (*Apology* LXVII)

From its infancy, the Christian Church has recognized not only the pastoral and theological praxis which underpins liturgical presidency, but has never attempted to isolate pastoral care and mission from the dynamics of leading worship.

The 'Social Capital' of Liturgy

This public and pastoral dimension is especially pertinent when account is taken of the positive consequences of the Church's liturgy beyond the immediate worshipping environment of the Church. The American sociologists Robert Putnam and David Campbell have recently identified the explicit influence which religious worship has on community cohesion (2010). A survey conducted in the United States between 2004 and 2006 identified worshipping communities as the locus of a significant degree of 'social capital'. Regular worshippers, defined not by the precise nature of their beliefs but by the frequency with which they inhabited a worshipping environment, are more likely to contribute to community cohesion through active citizenship.

Europe is a very different religious context from the USA, of course, with much higher levels of churchgoing and formal religious affiliation than is the case in Great Britain, for example. Nonetheless, Martyn Percy has written of the English situation as one where most people connect to the institutional church and its worship by 'relating and mutating' (2010, p. 52). The majority of the population may attend church rarely, if at all; but they still choose to maintain some kind of relationship, however distantly, to its rituals and buildings, through broadcasting or by memories and experiences. Such a relationship creates expectations, and Percy is one of a number commentators who argue for the (largely) unrestricted availability of the pastoral offices and counsel against the tendency for the Church's rituals – particularly those which mark significant life events – to become more specialized and detached from the 'mutating memory' of the population at large.[3]

Grace Davie, in identifying the steep decline in church attendance in Europe since the decade following the Second World War, has also acknowledged the increased growth taking place in the Church of England's cathedrals and other centres of liturgical excellence. This growth has coincided with a rise in the numbers of those undertaking pilgrimages (2006, p. 148). It suggests that, in a religious climate where many believe without belonging, there remains a residual hunger for the holy, which is being met through an imaginative and rigorous attitude towards the fundamental significance of worship in mission. It is not insignificant that cathedrals and similar churches are also key contributors to their cities and regions through social outreach and arts programmes, through the provision of education, as arenas for public discourse and as centres of pilgrimage.

At the heart of such worshipping communities is the liturgical president whose comportment expresses the Church's central *kerygma* in an unembarrassed and secure manner. The centrality of this embodied ministry has been identified by Robert Hovda as the foundational stance of those who preside at the liturgy:

In the liturgical assembly we are striving to be at the height of our God-consciousness, and therefore of our human consciousness. It is an awesome thing to face the mystery of the Other and the mystery of ourselves with such purpose and intent. It is intolerable that such an assembly should be led by a person who has no apparent interest in the proceedings,

---

3 See also, for example, Billings, 2010, esp. pp. 146–7.

or by a person who seems to be using the situation to dominate, or to display, or to collect the plaudits of the crowd.
(1986, p. 13)

Ritual Embarrassment: The Influence of Modernity on Western Culture

Such a disposition, which carries assumptions about the body,
space, the symbolic and other non-verbal features of life, is
not easily achieved – especially when account is taken of the
cultural and historical perspective from which the Church of
England's liturgical tradition emerged. A brief survey of this
milieu may reveal that it is often the unconscious source of the
embarrassment and even indifference, which can impede sensitive and intelligent liturgical presidency.

The Church of England's liturgy embodies a complex blend
of the catholic and the reformed. The Catholic culture of the
Middle Ages, which was displaced by the reformed worship
of the first Book of Common Prayer (1549), and the theology
which informed it was characterized by a high degree of artistic sophistication. Complex polyphonic music (epitomized by
the *Eton Choirbook*, c.1500–05); the choreographic intricacy
of the Sarum rite and other regional 'Uses'; the delicacy and
depth of art and iconography; and the multifaceted complexion of architecture, as well as the vividness of its colouration,
all combined to create a worshipping environment which was
multidimensional and highly sensorial. Worship, for the majority of the population, was experienced rather than understood. Language (whether it was 'understood' in a literal
sense or not) was just one element in a diverse and varied
collage of sights, sounds, smells, taste and touch, while numer-
ous strands of individual lay devotion flourished alongside the
Church's liturgy. There was space for the unconscious and
intuitive instincts to be brought into the liturgical arena. Even
when account is taken of the theological abuses (as well as the
political expediency) which paved the way for the abolition of

the medieval liturgy, it is possible to see that what character-ized much Christian worship on the cusp of the Reformation was a sense of the richness of human variety in relation to God. Referring to the multifarious nature of liturgical practice in the Middle Ages, its impact on the significant life events of society and individuals, as well as its capacity to shape the imagination of worshippers from cradle to grave, Eamon Duffy insists that

> Within that great seasonal cycle of fast and festival, of ritual observance and symbolic gesture, lay Christians found para-digms and stories which shaped their perception of the world and their place within it Within the liturgy: birth, copula-tion and death, journeying and homecoming, guilt and for-giveness, the blessing of homely things and the call to pass beyond them, were all located, tested and sanctioned. In the liturgy and in the sacramental celebration which were its central moments, mediaeval people found the key to the meaning and purpose of their lives. (1992, p. 11)

It is of no little significance, therefore, that those who are cur-rently seeking to provide appropriate forms of 'Fresh Expres-sions' worship in the Church of England, especially 'synthesis' worship geared to the needs of the un-churched in cathedrals and other large city-centre churches, are rediscovering the spatial, musical and symbolic dimensions of pre-Reformation worship alongside contemporary material.[4]

The Reformation, in its various manifestations, was charac-terized by Friedrich Schleiermacher as an era which sought greater certainty and tighter definition, where 'Everything mys-terious and marvellous is proscribed. Imagination is not to be filled . . . with airy images' (189). Worship gradually became more of a verbal and literary phenomenon. Music was dramati-cally simplified (with composers in England instructed to set one note to every syllable, for example, and the growth of simple

---

4 For an account of the way such liturgy functions as a primary vehi-cle of mission see Perham and Gray-Reeves (2011).

chorales and metrical psalms on the European mainland). Iconography and colour was depreciated (if not eradicated), and images were progressively replaced by texts. One of the gradual effects of The Book of Common Prayer, with its particular concern for uniformity alongside the provision of liturgy in the vernacular, was to make worship rational: meaning was more precisely mapped-out. What was intended to be liberating became, in significant ways, more specific and containing.

The philosophical, political and cultural developments which continued from the Reformation towards the emergence of the Enlightenment, which witnessed the flourishing of individual human rights, greater intellectual freedom, democracy and an openness to scientific method, also contributed to a persistent devaluing of revelation, imagination, symbol and metaphor. It was an age in which bureaucracy, as well as religious scepticism, flourished; where the non-analytical and non-profit-making contribution of music, poetry, art and, significantly, religious ritual, to cultural intelligence was marginalized. The unfettered power of the Church was replaced by the all-imposing power of the state.

In pictorial terms, the camera image became prized over, say, the classical icon or an impressionistic painting. The drive for clarity and precision of expression resulted in a culture where language, especially public language, assumed a mechanistic and literal character. The Romantic movement may have succeeded in offering a counter-balance (especially in reaction to the impact of the precise, mechanistic and symmetrical world of the Industrial Revolution), as it sought to recover the value of beauty and a sense of the numinous. Nonetheless, the educational, scientific and philosophical culture we have inherited is one in which the objective, calculable and measurable world is more highly valued than the intuitive, subjective, metaphorical and symbolic dimensions of life. It is no accident, for example, that the style of Christian worship which developed during this period sought to objectify belief through linguistic precision and dispensed with the musical, symbolic and architectural dimensions essential to a previous era. It was, significantly, also an age in which the seeds of significant strands of modern Christian fundamentalism were first sown and where the notion of 'reading the service' was first expressed.

Recovering a Suppressed Dimension

One particularly engaging (and properly controversial) response to this cultural and philosophical situation, which has considerable implications for presiding at the Church's liturgy, can be found in the recent work of the English psychiatrist Iain McGilchrist (2009). Drawing on the insights of neurological science in relation to an analysis of Western cultural history, McGilchrist argues that Westerners have sleep-walked over the course of recent centuries into suppressing the right hemisphere of the brain in favour of the left. Instead of co-operating, the right and left hemispheres of the brain are engaged in a struggle for power, and many aspects of contemporary Western culture reflect – and have contributed to – the left's dominance over the right.

Put simply, McGilchrist argues that because the world we inhabit today prizes the left hemisphere's preference for the logical, analytical, abstract and mathematical over the intuitive, artistic and individually specific, it is no surprise that the right hemisphere has become a 'silent partner'. This has distorted a thoroughly synoptic vision of reality. Because the relationship between the two hemispheres of the brain is significant for the type of world we inhabit

> many important aspects of experience, those that the right hemisphere is particularly well equipped to deal with – our passions, our sense of humour, all metaphoric and symbolic understanding (and with it the symbolic and metaphoric nature of art), all religious sense, all imaginative and intuitive processes – [are rendered explicit by the left hemisphere and become] 'mechanical, lifeless'. (p. 209)

Do You See?

One potentially fruitful (and challenging) aspect of McGilchrist's work for liturgical presidents relates to his insight about how the brain brings reality into focus and deals with the human capacity to 'image' the implicit and explicit. The brain's left hemisphere, according to McGilchrist, produces an illusion of clarity because it is concerned with the explicit: with what is seen on the surface. The eye looks at something, and the brain's left hemisphere 'returns us to what we already know' (p. 180). This suppresses the capacity for sustained attention, the ability to see something new and be delighted by the unexpected or weakens the capacity to see through and around the object that is seen. This is what makes the implicit and implied opaque, and vision is reduced to the two-dimensional plane.

The right hemisphere of the brain, by contrast, is equipped to deal with depth and the capacity to see beyond the object under scrutiny. It brings the one who sees into relationship with what the eye sees and allows for a significant degree of transparency. This dimension of depth, argues McGilchrist, is significant for psychological health because schizophrenia, for example, which imitates an over-active left hemisphere, is characterized by a loss of perspective and an inability to engage with the broader perspective (see p. 183).

Significantly for those who preside at the liturgy, this loss of depth and perspective is what makes drama alienating, precisely because it is reduced to 'a picture in which we do not participate' (p. 184). What makes good drama absorbing, by contrast, is a transparency or translucence where the actors and the playwright are not the focus of attention:

> That's why bad acting can be so embarrassing. It draws our attention to the fact that the actors are acting, and to how they see themselves; they become like critics whose self-preening causes them to obtrude between us and what they claim to illuminate. The implicit becomes explicit and all is lost. (p. 184)

The left hemisphere's preference for the explicit needs to be counter-balanced by the right hemisphere's capacity to treat the actors as semi-transparent, which allows some engagement with the living reality of the character they embody, so that they seem to melt away into the characters and the drama they are representing.

Technology and Anonymity

Drama is an observed and experienced activity. Words are not simply read off a page or a screen in an environment detached from the person who produced those words. They are heard and delivered with a particular tone and register of the voice. We see the face of the person who speaks those words, witness their body language and have some insight into their character. We observe the life-setting from which those words emerge and may even have some notion of how the situation will develop. The words may be surrounded by (or set to) music, and there may be a pictorial or symbolic backdrop. The Industrial Revolution and the technological developments which followed in its wake have reduced the embodied character of human communication. The invention of the printing press, which was to prove so decisive for the realization of the Reformation, enabled words to be encountered in isolation from the person who wrote or spoke them. Admittedly, even in more ancient societies it was possible to send disembodied words, as edicts were proclaimed, orders issued and laws enforced by distant monarchs; but these were often accompanied by physical 'presences' such as symbols, seals and signatures and often verbally declaimed by a herald with all the potential for register of voice and facial expression to convey nuance and depth.

Nonetheless, we now find ourselves inhabiting a world where information technology has disembodied the way individuals and institutions communicate, with email being the emblematic epitome of how words are transmitted at speed, without emotion, gesture, vocal timbre or, very often, consideration of how they will be received. One of the consequences of the technological revolution which has accompanied the development of the internet is that words are transmitted with no surrounding context, but in one-dimensional horizontal lines, devoid of 'vertical' depth. As McGilchrist has identified, the history of the evolution of writing has witnessed a move from the vertical to the horizontal which had, essentially, been completed over four millennia ago; and the right hemisphere of the brain's preference for the vertical has been subsumed by the left hemisphere's preference for the horizontal (p. 276).

The American Methodist scholar, Susan White, has observed how this 'horizontal' preference has resulted in mechanistic (and mechanized) expectations of the liturgy. For example, many Roman Catholics have experienced several decades of 'globalized' liturgy through the production of the weekly 'missalette', where the shape and content of the liturgy has been imposed by the apparent convenience of having a publishing house provide their preferred version of the rite. Other denominations have been similarly burdened by the profusion of liturgical source-books and software packages, which allow texts to be cut and pasted, or what White calls 'cannibalized', from their original context and transplanted into new liturgical bodies. The potential for this to be done without theological, pastoral or cultural discernment is considerable, and feeds the expectation that liturgy is primarily about printed texts, rather than a more complex reality in which other, non-textual dimensions are of equal import.

> This sort of technological approach to the building of liturgical systems means that there has been an additional need to eliminate as much friction as possible from the worship components. The parts must somehow be made to work smoothly, and the quality of the resulting product must be predictable and (ideally) of uniform quality. (1994, p. 104)

What Does it Mean?

This neurological and technological perspective is significant in explaining how reality became defined in the historical and cultural momentum which has accompanied the evolution of the Church of England's worship since the mid-sixteenth century. As McGilchrist has identified, what characterized the Reformation and the Enlightenment can be interpreted as a triumph of the left hemisphere over the right, where we find

> banishment of wonder, the triumph of the explicit, and, with it, mistrust of metaphor, alienation from the embodied world of the flesh, and a consequent cerebralization of life and experience. The right hemisphere's bid for reason, in which opposites can be held in balance, was swiftly transformed into a move toward left-hemisphere rationality, in which one of the two must exclude, even annihilate, the other. (2009, p. 337)

The evolving worshipping environment, which championed the explicit proclamation of the word over the implicit, embodied, dramatic and symbolic dimensions, has allowed liturgy to become a two-dimensional phenomenon, where the non-verbal, non-literary elements of liturgy must 'mean' something and be, somehow, self-explanatory if they are to have a place. A prevalent attitude towards the re-discovery (and often selective) use of the symbolic dimensions of worship is that it is acceptable just as long as it can be explained and interpreted – and if it cannot, it is the president's task to interpret, explain, translate and impose its meaning on worshippers. McGilchrist observes: 'The left hemisphere misunderstands the importance of explicitness' (p. 345). The implications of this insight in relation to liturgical language will be discussed in more detail in Chapter 3.

Addressing such insights is of critical importance to those who are called to preside at the Church's liturgy precisely because we cannot ignore the cultural and philosophical assumptions which have shaped us. 'You are' (in Augustine of Hippo's telling aphorism) 'what you have received' – and, by implication, we give to others what we have already received. To acknowledge the multi-layered dimension of our human and cultural development and to admit what has implicitly (and explicitly) entered our consciousness, will necessarily inform what Paul Ricoeur called a 'hermeneutic of suspicion' in confronting those influences which could easily reduce worship to a mere reflection of ourselves and the world we know.

What worship discloses to those who worship and what the liturgical president is called to embody and communicate is a keen sense that the language, symbols and gestures of the liturgy can enable epiphany: not an anthropocentric confection contrived to collude with present cultural expectations, but an incursion of the divine into a moment of human history, shaped by the experience and insights of the whole sweep of Judeo-Christian history. How the insights of history might impinge on the self-understanding of the liturgical president's calling and task will be explored in the next chapter.

Inclinations

For now, it is worth pondering an insight of the American Presbyterian minister, Kimberly Bracken Long, who has written of the necessity for those who preside at the Church's liturgy to possess an 'inclination of mystery' (2009, p. 2). This inclination goes against the grain of many post-Reformation, post-Enlightenment cultural assumptions; and, in the light of McGilchrist's insights, might be identified as the locus of the human struggle to perceive reality. This touches on the primary importance of the liturgical president's spirituality, self-awareness and capacity to enable others to glimpse something of what s/he has already seen of the holy. If those who preside at the liturgy are ambivalent about

its capacity to meet the needs of those in search of an enc
with the holy or feel embarrassment at the cultural strar
of the gestures and symbols which convey something of the reality of the divine presence, worship will be encumbered from the
outset by the president's inner and outer comportment.

> One who is convinced that symbol and reality are mutually
> exclusive should avoid the liturgy. Such a one should also
> avoid poetry, concerts and the theatre, language, loving
> another person, and most other attempts at communicating
> with one's kind. Symbol is reality at its most intense degree of
> being expressed. One resorts to symbol when reality swamps
> all other forms of discourse. This happens regularly when one
> approaches God with others, as in the liturgy. Symbol is thus
> as native to liturgy as metaphor is to language. One learns to
> live with symbol and metaphor or gives up the ability to speak
> or to worship communally. (Kavanagh, 1982/90, p. 103)

If the presider fundamentally believes that the divine can be
mediated through drama and song, spaces and signs (many of
which have their origins in a very different cultural milieu) and
is committed to investing the intellectual and spiritual energy
to ensure that these dimensions are given confident expression,
the worship of the people of God stands a chance of becoming a lively arena in which worshippers are drawn ever more
deeply into the mysteries of faith.

This is why good liturgical presidency can never simply be
reduced to the acquisition of techniques and skills. Nor will
it be fundamentally enabled merely in the provision of time,
money and greater priority in patterns of training.

> Liturgy is unique among human assemblies in its direct con-
> cern with ultimate issues and the totality of life . . . a conviction
> about the importance of liturgical action are assets that a pre-
> sider can neither feign nor do without. (Hovda, 1986, p. 8)

More than 'Here and Now'

Those 'ultimate issues' are an indication of the presider's role in evoking, from inner conviction, an environment in which the reality of God (which is both immanent and transcendent), can be acknowledged and celebrated. In short, it is paramount that those who preside at the Church's liturgy have a keenly developed sense that the worship at which they preside is somehow an active and urgent participation in the realities of this world – and the world that is to come. This fundamental conviction is a crucial necessity, if worship is to be more than a mirror-image of the cultural status quo, where any sense of the reality of God as Other has become marginalized. This touches on some basic notions of what makes Christian worship – and liturgical presidency – *authentic*. It is what helps to orientate the presider's focus resolutely away from him/herself and raises the expectations of those who come to worship that the activity in which they are engaged begins decisively with God. It enables liturgical presidency (in Graham Hughes' striking image) to become a 'boundary' event:

> it takes place at a kind of virtual 'edge' of what we can manage conceptually and emotionally . . . the event is nullified if it is permitted (as it threatens constantly to do) to fall back into domesticity or 'routinization'. (2003, p. 301)

More than 'Me'

Questions of authenticity also inevitably become concentrated on the president as a *persona*. This is especially so when the call to preside at the liturgy is identified in relation to the priest being *in loco Christi* and a public representative of the Church – historically as well as contemporaneously. This privilege is almost always bound up with anxieties about striving to be one's 'true self' in the face of the demands of being a representative person, authorized to a particular ministry, which requires much more than simply being 'myself'. This is a dimension of the president's distinctive calling which is notoriously difficult to express.

Hovda, for example, struggles to name how a liturgical president can be 'present' without eclipsing the presence of Christ, by feeling for an appropriate level of 'consciousness . . . awareness' (1986, p. 1). Kavanagh advises presidents to place themselves 'in the background', so that attention is focused on Christ as God's living word 'rather than one's own virtuosity' (1982/90, p. 94). This is just a hint at the insufficiency of a presidential stance which prizes the notion of merely 'being me' over and against the challenge to become 'more than me'. This not only relates to the dynamics of embodying the momentum of a living tradition, in the words spoken and gestures employed; it also poses the challenge of how the experience of presiding at the liturgy can be sufficiently transformative, so that a president (and the congregation being led in worship) is somehow 'enlarged' by the inhabiting of the role. When this is properly understood, good presidency will be seen not so much in terms of 'this is how I like to do it' or 'this is what works for me', but 'these are the accumulated insights of the Church, gleaned from the wisdom and experience of those who have contributed to shaping its worship over several millennia and to which I am now called to give authentic and imaginative expression'.

This is a stance which William Seth Adams describes as 'impersonation' (1995, p. 27). The one who impersonates (not to caricature satirically but to allow the character of something other than the self to be impressed and imprinted on the self) becomes a conduit for the fullness of Christian tradition. To preside by 'impersonation' is to be both oneself *and* much more than oneself. It signifies how worship is a transformative activity where all worshippers are called to be more than themselves in the expression of their praise, penitence, thanksgiving, generosity and desire for justice. It is the president's task to raise the expectation in all who worship that 'something more' is always possible – in what is hoped for, given and received. This is just one way in which presiding at the Eucharist assumes a sacramental character and relates specifically to cultivating those repeated habits which will form, re-form and inform a president's spirituality. In the final chapter, I offer some hints and suggestions about what those habits might involve.

Entertainment Transfigured by Enchantment?

Given the cultural momentum which has accompanied the development of the Church of England's liturgy, such an orientation will pose challenges, underscore opportunities and provoke a re-examination of our roots to inform authentic and imaginative liturgical celebration for the present and the future. In particular, it highlights the degree to which the liturgical president is able to challenge the way in which accumulated cultural assumptions have resulted in a restraining of theological horizons, where rationality and functionality have overshadowed a sense of the implicit and mysterious. A renewed sense of confidence in the task and calling of the liturgical president could potentially enable the Church to use more complex and intricate language, symbolism, space and music to widen the horizons of those who worship (whether rarely or regularly) and to open their lives to the all-embracing love of the God who is beyond rational restraint or cultural confinement. Worship, as David Brown has remarked,

> has . . . to be seen as more than just a matter of strengthening the community for mission and service. At its heart lies the adoration of God, basking in his presence in and for its own sake. Failing to acknowledge that deeper dimension to liturgy, though, is part of a much wider malaise . . . that is the general retreat of theology . . . from numerous other areas of human life. (2004, p. 20)

I began this chapter by highlighting the complexity of the 'baggage' which liturgical presidents embody and the historical, personal, theological and ecclesial awareness which should underpin the calling which priests and other liturgical ministers have embraced. In the following chapter, some of those historical and theological factors will be brought into focus in an attempt to challenge some previously held presuppositions about the nature of Eucharistic celebration, and to encourage contemporary presidents to explore how a renewed understanding of the history and development of the Church's defining act of worship might influence their own approach to presiding at it today.

2

Temple or Home, Table or Altar, Supper or Sacrifice? Tradition in Transition

The witness of the New Testament is . . . twofold: it transcends the land, Jerusalem, the Temple. Yes: but its history and theology demand a concern with these realities also. Is there a reconciling principle in these apparently contradictory attitudes? (Davies, 1974, p. 367)

There is no more a possibility of escape from a tradition than there is the possibility of an escape from history or language. (Tracy, 1988, p. 16)

Presiding at the Eucharist is an activity which inescapably connects presidents and those they lead in worship to other times, other places, other world-views and to that ultimate Other: the reality of God. The liturgy at which a president presides today has taken centuries in coming to be. In this chapter, I want to suggest that competent presidency carries, however implicitly, a keen awareness of the historical dynamics as well as a grasp of the development of the Christian tradition, which informs our understanding of the Eucharist today. By having some familiarity with the broad outline of the landscape of history and tradition and by looking afresh at some previously unquestioned assumptions, presidents may be better equipped to consider questions such as:

- What am I doing when I prepare to preside at the Church's central act of worship – and what defining events and ideas have shaped my preparation for, and understanding of, the task and role entrusted to me?

- How is my pattern of presiding influenced by the historic, cultural and theological evolution of the Eucharist?
- How does this influence enable me to make informed and imaginative choices concerning gesture, text, space and symbol to enable the Eucharist celebration to be an authentic expression of the faith of the Church?

Underlying these questions is a complex tapestry of theology, history, controversy, social and political influences, personal preferences, guesswork – and a good measure of misunderstanding. Presidents may be aware of the tradition in which they stand, may be clear about what events and ideas have informed that tradition over time, may be aware of practices which inform other traditions and even be willing to absorb what they consider to be good about those practices. Nonetheless, history and tradition are never static and the elapse of time often allows new insights and discoveries to come into focus.

Perceptions of Tradition

It is easy to caricature different theological and ecclesial traditions and, broadly speaking, the prevailing assumption has been that, for Anglicans, certain traits can be identified which define a particular theological and ecclesiastical stance.

Those who feel most comfortable in Protestant and Evangelical territory, for example, will be keenly aware of the principles which informed the Reformers' distinctive (and diverse) understanding of the Eucharist. This may include the need for personal conviction and sincerity – by both president and worshippers – coupled to the expectation that there is worthy reception of the sacrament. The one who presides is expected to possess a sufficient degree of learning, not least in the interpretation of the scriptures. The words spoken and sung should be faithful to scriptural revelation. A sense of the word being made explicit in the celebration of the sacrament and clarity of meaning are underlying priorities. Music, symbolism and movement may be part of the celebration, but are rarely essential. There is a clear expectation that the liturgy, in whatever form, will clearly focus on the commemoration of the Last Supper and the saving benefits of Christ's sacrifice on the cross.

By contrast, those whose preferred environment is Catholic will be concerned that the language and actions of the liturgy have some continuity with the historic practice of the Church, as well as a degree of connection with contemporary Catholic practice (the rubrics and gestures of the Roman rite are often a point of reference if not prescription). It is expected that those who preside should embody catholic continuity (particularly through the manner of their ordination) and their theological stance should provide a measure of sacramental 'assurance'. A sense that the divine is mediated and becomes incarnated through physical things (especially the consecrated bread and wine) and through bodily actions in worship is a strong undercurrent. There is a keen sense of *anamnesis* in the sense of a dynamic recalling and reliving of the sacrifice of the cross, as well as a belief in the real presence of Christ in the consecrated elements.

Others, voicing different degrees of catholic and reformed insight, will be keen to ensure that the liturgy expresses contemporary concerns, specific social and ethical issues, making the language and symbols of the liturgy accessible and meaningful to particular categories of people and specific cultures, as well as those who will expect no discernible departure from an unchanging practice dating back to a specific period in history – however recent!

Nonetheless, superficial attempts to define different traditions and identify their characteristics rarely tell the whole story. A willingness to re-evaluate some previously unquestioned assumptions, coupled to an appreciation that history and scholarship is always revealing new insights, can prove much more fruitful – and liberate us from partial allegiances and perspectives.

Supper at the Table?

We can reasonably expect that, for most Christians, the celebration of the Eucharist is rooted in the command of Jesus to his followers, at the Last Supper, to 'do this in remembrance of me'. These words, which are common to the all three synoptic Gospel accounts (Matt. 26.17ff; Mark 14.12ff; Luke 22.7ff) and Paul's account of the Last Supper (1 Cor. 11.23–6), would appear to possess a measure of consistency in their *general* detail. How they were first heard and handed on by the earliest Christians, how they have been interpreted over the evolving course of Christian history and what their implications are for an understanding of Eucharistic worship today raises some interesting questions.

A good starting place for contemporary presidents might be to ask: what is the connection between the Last Supper, the way the first generation of Christians understood the Eucharist and the way the Eucharist might be celebrated today?

One strand of scholarship, drawing on the synoptic Gospel accounts, argues for a clear connection between the Last Supper and the Jewish Passover. The work of N. T. Wright (1996)[1] is representative of this approach. It has provided weight to those who argue in favour of a domestic rather than public setting for our Eucharistic origins, intimate rather than grand in scale. That the earliest Christian communities worshipped in a domestic setting is often cited as a consequence of the Passover setting for the Last Supper – especially when account is taken of the long tradition of a domestic celebration in Jerusalem prior to the reforms of King Josiah (*c.*623 BC and chronicled in 2 Kings 23) and Jewish practice after the destruction of the Temple (70 CE).

Another strand of scholarship argues that, because the synoptic Gospel (and Paul's) accounts differ in *specific* detail, they

---

1 Wright states that the accounts of the Last Supper draw the conclusion that it was 'virtually certain that the meal in question was *some kind* of Passover meal' (1996, p. 555).

need to be viewed through the lens of the liturgical practices of the early Christian communities, which undoubtedly influenced their final written form. In other words, the Last Supper needs to be understood in relation to other occasions of table fellowship in the Gospels. Such an approach highlights not so much the existence of the DNA of a single historic reality, but rather the contrasting strands of emphasis provided by the New Testament writers. Building on the work of Rudolph Bultmann (1952), Dominic Crossan suggests that the Last Supper may have been a less defining event in the early Christian consciousness than is usually assumed:

> Jesus and those closest to him would have had a last supper . . . a meal that later and in retrospect was recognised as having been their last together . . . I do not presume any distinctive meal known before hand, designated specifically, or ritually programmed as final and forever . . . It is also necessary to calculate very carefully what was lost and gained in moving from Jesus' real meal with open commensality to its continuance in a ritual meal with Christian commensality. (1991, pp. 361, 367)

No Last Supper on Maundy Thursday?

One source of evidence for early Christian liturgical practice in Jerusalem is the dairy of Egeria, a nun from Galicia, who made a pilgrimage to Jerusalem in the final decades of the fourth century. She describes the worship of Holy Week, particularly in relation to the historic sites. She speaks of two Eucharistic celebrations on Maundy Thursday but, significantly, not in relation to the site of the Last Supper. In a lengthy account of the events of the day, Egeria describes how everyone hurries home after the second Eucharist for supper, so that they are free to return for the major celebrations at the Eleona church, the traditional site of the cave in the Garden of Gethsemane. This may suggest that the Church in Jerusalem in the fourth century saw little direct link between the place of the Last Supper, the institution of the Eucharist and the development of the Eucharist as an act of worship in the post-Constantinian Church:

> Egeria makes no reference to the Last Supper on Holy Thursday . . . Before the end of the Fourth Century no effort had been made to pinpoint the location of the Last Supper or to integrate it into the Jerusalem liturgy. Rather the Holy Sepulchre complex served as the locus of the celebration . . . And so the whole celebration formed a sort of *inclusion* beginning and ending at this complex. The motivation here was just as ecclesial as it is historical. (Baldovin, 1987, pp. 87–8)

Chicken and Egg: Dual Origins?

Liturgical scholars have long espoused the so-called 'dual hypothesis' approach to our Eucharistic origins. This suggests that, broadly speaking, two ritual meals evolved in the early decades of Christian history. One was a fellowship meal, usually comprising bread and wine – and it should be remembered that, in the ancient world, these two elements were often sufficient ingredients for an occasion to be called a meal. This was a less formal and more frequent meal and has, broadly, been identified as the *agape* (conventionally translated as 'love feast'). It was an event which could be celebrated by any gathering of Christians. The other was a more formal event, over which an authorized person presided. The bread and cup were specifically linked to the body and blood of Jesus Christ. This event contained the reading of the scriptures, the offering of prayers and gifts (bread, wine and often money as well as other symbols of productivity), thanksgiving over the bread and cup and the sharing of the elements – both within and beyond the assembly. This is what has come to be called the *Eucharist*.

This method of accounting for early Eucharistic development assumes that all Christians ate their 'cultic' meals for specifically defined reasons, in precise ways, using recognized texts, and were consistent in their description and understanding of them. Straightforward assumptions about two broad strands of development are not easily achieved when account is taken of the cultural shift from the Jewish world into the Graeco-Roman world. As Andrew McGowan has argued, account needs to be taken not only of the Hellenistic impact on Jewish ritual meals, especially among the diaspora communities in places to which Christianity also spread, but also of the cultural and religious assumptions which predominated in the societies in which early Christianity took root. How these distinctive meals and rituals were described and understood depends, to a large degree, on who is describing them and interpreting them (Jewish, Christian or Pagan). The ingredients of these meals and rituals were not universally uniform (not simply bread *and* wine, but sometimes without wine, sometimes including fish, milk and honey as well as other local foodstuffs), and differing degrees of significance will have been attached to them depending on the geographical and cultural context (McGowan, 2010).

It may be reasonable to assume that early Christian identity was bound up with rituals focused on eating and drinking; it is less certain how and when, precisely, a communal fellowship meal assumed sacramental significance. As I shall highlight below (p. 45), because attention needs to be given to the diversity of early Eucharistic practice, as well as the emergence of different expressions of Christianity in different locations at different times, caution is necessary when it comes to accepting that two easily delineated strands of ritual developed side by side in a uniform pattern. A mode of 'meshing' and 'morphing' might be more probable – especially if early Christian liturgical practice can be understood in relation to the doctrinal diversity that often characterized different Christian communities in different locations, where belief developed over time before it became credally defined.

Weekly or Annually?

Alongside the broad acceptance of the dual hypothesis of Eucharistic development, there has been a prevailing assumption that the Eucharist was a weekly event: the Lord's command enacted on the Lord's Day. However, Christians never adopted the Jewish Sabbath and the earliest descriptions of early Eucharistic practice are far from unequivocal in stating how frequently the Eucharist was celebrated. Taking a broadly sociological approach, Martin Stringer has argued that the Eucharist, as we now recognize it, was not established as a weekly liturgical event until the beginning of the second century CE. He suggests that what is described in 1 Corinthians 11 is more likely to have been an annual commemorative meal, linking the Passover and Last Supper, as described in the passion narratives in the Gospels (2011). There is a significant lack of proof for the Last Supper providing the basis for a weekly act of worship until evidence emerges in Rome in the first decades of the second century, through the writings of Ignatius of Antioch (d. *c.*110 CE) and other contemporary personalities. Stringer explores the development of the Christian commemoration of the Last Supper in relation to meals and table fellowship in the Jewish and Pagan cultures in which Christianity spread. Recognizing their sacrificial character, as well as their significance in public and social life, he identifies how evidence for particular practices in specific places was first transmitted orally before written texts were developed.

The question of whether the Eucharist was originally a weekly or annual celebration points towards another area of investigation: what is the defining event which shaped the development and understanding of the Eucharist in the first century of the Christian era? Was it simply the annual domestic celebration of Passover; or might it have been more consciously the annual sacrifice in the Temple on the Day of Atonement?

Sacrifice in the Temple?

This is a question which has exercised biblical and liturgical scholars who have identified a lack of continuity between the Passover, the Last Supper and the development of the Eucharist. They stress the degree to which early, non-biblical, Christian texts make no link between the Eucharist and the Last Supper. The most obvious example of these is the *Didache*, a Greek text which probably originated in Syria, variously dated between the middle of the first and second centuries CE. It provides one of the earliest written sources of Christian Eucharistic liturgy, but contains no material from the scriptural accounts of the Last Supper – despite the unmistakably Jewish character of its prayers over the bread and cup.

Margaret Barker, in particular, has argued persuasively (if controversially) that the pivotal Jewish influence on the development of early Christian Eucharistic liturgies is not so much the domestic setting of the Passover, but the more ritually elaborate Temple rite on the Day of Atonement (2008, esp. chapter 7). Barker also suggests that the Temple ritual which shaped the early Christian liturgical imagination was not the Temple Jesus knew, but its pre-exilic predecessor and the persistently preserved memories of its pre-reformed liturgy by Jesus' Jewish contemporaries. Barker argues that much of the language, imagery and expectation articulated in the New Testament is focused on the *renewal* of the covenant enacted in the first Temple. As I will highlight below (p. 52), Barker's argument could have a significant bearing on our understanding of what influenced the development of early liturgical practice and how this might inform and inspire a re-imagining of how the Eucharist might be celebrated in our contemporary context.

The examples and questions I have cited have implications, not only for our understanding of the origins of the Eucharist and its historical development, but also for the liturgical, theological and aesthetic considerations of those who preside at the Eucharist today. They highlight the degree to which the spatial setting of the Eucharist, its language, gestures, symbols, colours, sounds and movements are all of a piece with how we understand its early evolution. Certainly, they underline the insufficiency of assuming that the experience of Jesus and his first followers was simply the liturgically minimalist environment of home and synagogue or that there is clear-cut continuity between the way Christians celebrate the Eucharist today and what happened in the upper room on the night before Jesus was crucified. Rather, we need to investigate the character and momentum of our Eucharistic origins in order to realize the Eucharist's centrality, both for the mission of the contemporary Church as well as the formation of Christian communities.

Formal or Improvised? Fixed or Fluid?

To ask how the first generations of Christians worshipped or how Jesus and his Jewish contemporaries worshipped is a vexed and potentially frustrating question. Recent liturgical scholarship has emphasized the improvisatory nature of early Christian worship and the diversity of practice from place to place (Bradshaw, 2004, esp. chapters 4 and 5). However, it is important not to impose a twenty-first-century understanding of what 'improvised' or 'diverse' might mean on to a religious culture that was wholly unlike the postmodern, individualist, celebrity-obsessed, religiously sceptic culture of the Northern hemisphere in the twenty-first century. There are several reasons why a measure of caution, as well as openness to different historical and cultural perspectives, will prove advantageous.

First, few written forms of Christian liturgy exist prior to the fourth century. This is not simply because the earliest Christians were a persecuted minority who were anxious to avoid written 'evidence' of their cultic activities; or because the majority of those living in the ancient Middle East and Mediterranean were largely illiterate; or even because the domestic spatial setting of early Christian worship lent itself more readily to an informal style. More likely is the possibility that Jews at the time of Jesus were discouraged (and, in some teachings, forbidden) from making written copies of their liturgy. The first known complete Jewish liturgical book was not published until 875 CE, for example. Despite the many ways in which Christianity soon came to represent a radical departure from its Jewish roots, the Jewish character of Christian worship is clearly identifiable. Therefore, it seems unlikely that the first generation of Christians would have so fundamentally departed from such a characteristic of the worshipping tradition they had inherited – particularly when the cultures into which Christianity spread from its native Jewish soil were largely aural in character.

It is worth emphasizing the centrality of aural tradition in the Middle Eastern cultures to which Christianity first spread and some of its basic characteristics. It is most obviously encountered, today, in the Islamic *medrassa*, where the entire *Qu'ran* is committed to memory; where written copies of the scripture often play an inconspicuous role. In some oriental orthodox churches of the East, for example, extensive and complex liturgies are memorized by the clergy, and printed texts are rarely provided. Kenneth Bailey (2008) has suggested that this methodology was not only employed in rabbinic tradition at the time of Jesus, but remains a feature of Middle Eastern communities today. It is characterized by a dynamic interdependence of informality and control. Whether the context is an informal gathering (of villagers in a social setting, for example) or in a more formal educational arena, there is a commitment to *faithful preservation* of a store of narratives, wisdom and poetry. Because the transmission takes place in *public*, the community provides a means of collective control and self-regulation over any departure from faithful retelling. There is a basic assumption that the teacher, the storyteller or an individual within the community will not change or manipulate what is being transmitted without the consent of the whole community who hears it – especially where it concerns scripture or collective wisdom. It is significant, therefore, that the rabbinic figure of Paul should begin his retelling of the Last Supper in such a spirit: 'I received from the Lord what I also handed on to you' as a device to claim (and reclaim) authenticity (1 Cor. 11.17ff).

Second, there is a body of evidence to suggest that, while early Christian worship was characterized by variety, a *general* measure of consensus seems to have been achieved towards the end of first century of the Christian Era. The context of Paul's retelling of the Last Supper, for example, was a Christian community whose liturgical and ethical practice was deemed to have fundamentally departed from an identifiable pattern. Justin Martyr (d. 167 CE) provides one of the earliest descriptions of a Sunday celebration of the Eucharist in his *First Apology*, and although he writes that the one who presides 'gives thanks in his own way' (*Apology* 67), his description clearly identifies a basic ritual shape with key elements, suggesting that they were well-established (the kiss of peace, the presentation of bread and wine mixed with water, the Trinitarian character of the prayers and so forth). Tertullian (*c.*160–225 CE) writing in North Africa also describes well-established traditions, including the elements of a rite which contained intercessory prayer (with a particular emphasis on the social order), scriptural readings, exhortation and the giving of alms to particular needs (*Apology* 39). Although he describes a separate 'supper' in the same source which is manifestly not a Eucharist (and uses *agape* to describe – and differentiate? – it from a Eucharist), elsewhere Tertullian writes of early-morning gatherings where the 'sacrament' of the Eucharist was received 'from the hands of none but the president' (*De Corona* 3). The Alexandrian bishop Origen (*c.*185–251 CE), like Tertullian, uses the word 'Eucharist' to refer specifically to the bread set aside for liturgical use and even provides explicit instructions about not discarding fragments of the consecrated bread. He also uses language resonant of the *Didache* to describe the central act of taking and blessing bread (*Contra Celsum* 8.33).

Third, evidence of a written liturgical form (such as the *Didache*) should not automatically indicate uniformity of practice. When exploring the historic origins and development of Christian liturgy, account must be taken of how the shape, language and theology of the liturgy might have been experienced in different places at different times. It should not be assumed, for example, that the faith was received and expressed in identical ways in different cities and regions or that it developed at the same pace and in the same way. The discovery of primitive 'Church Orders' cannot provide definitive conclusions about the shape and content of Christian worship at a particular place and time.

This corresponds with present-day experience and evidence. Commenting on the contemporary inculturation of the liturgy, Anscar Chapungco (1989) suggests that, in the current authorized Roman Catholic liturgy, we may have a basic script for the liturgy; but it is not the liturgy *as it is actually celebrated* in countless particular communities across the world. It is adapted to various cultural, spatial and social circumstances. Anyone visiting those communities (whether in the same country, diocese or locality), would encounter diversity of practice and emphasis. This is commensurate with our experience of an aspect of contemporary domestic life. A brief survey of a representative sample of recipe books by celebrity chefs, for example, might give the impression that most British people in the second decade of the twenty-first century eat a diet of locally sourced, fresh, seasonal food, cooked at home, using specific recipes and methods, eaten in particular social gatherings (dinner parties, Sunday lunch around the family dining table, a barbecue with the neighbours, etc.). The reality is manifestly very different! The possession of textual evidence for a model – liturgical or otherwise – should not lead to the conclusion that it is evidence for actual or even uniform practice.

Fourth, a body of evidence exists to suggest that the liturgy was a primary means of Christian formation. The composition of the First Letter of Peter, for example, has been identified as a mystagogical reflection on the early baptismal rites at Easter (Cross, 1954). Personalities such as Basil of Caesarea (*c.*330–79 CE) referred in his writing to 'mysteries' which manifestly concerned worship (e.g. *On the Holy Spirit*, esp. pp. 66–7) where the significance of liturgical practice was given a degree of emphasis. The mystagogical *Catechesis* of Cyril of Jerusalem also reflects this practice. He takes the liturgical practices of baptism (*Catecheses* 3 and 21), the Eucharist (22) and 'On the Sacred Liturgy and Communion' (23) as well as extensive interrogation of the articles of the Nicene Creed as the basis for instructing new converts who were experiencing these rites. This suggests that a basic liturgical pattern was not only established, but deemed sufficiently universal in character to be placed alongside settled creedal statements.

Fifth, it is a perennial temptation, when engaged in any examination of ancient texts, to impose a framework which has been fashioned by the perspective and world-view from which we examine them. In short, it can be all too easy to find what you are looking for!

One celebrated example is the work of the Anglican Benedictine Gregory Dix (1901–52) whose *Shape of the Liturgy* (1945) was profoundly influential, not only for Anglican liturgical scholarship right up to the 1980s, but also impacted considerably on the process of Anglican liturgical revision in England and other Anglican provinces, culminating in the publication of the *Alternative Service Book* in 1980. Dix's identification of a 'four-fold' shape underpinning the textual diversity of the earliest Eucharistic rites has been the subject of a sustained critique in recent decades, because his historical method was seen as being too heavily influenced by a selective reading of the available data, as well as his own monastic community's preference for the Roman rite (see Spinks, 1990). Another example is Josef Jungmann's monumental re-appraisal of the origins of the Roman rite, which contributed significantly to the reform of the Roman Catholic liturgy following the Second Vatican Council. Not only did Jungmann's insights emerge at a time when the Roman Catholic Church was beginning to acknowledge significant aspects of the prevailing Protestant critique of later Medieval Christianity; there were also significant liturgical consequences arising from his reading of the history of the development of the Roman rite.

One example is the (virtually unchallengeable) proliferation of the offertory procession in modern Western Eucharistic liturgies, in which lay worshippers carry the bread and wine to the altar as a sign that the whole people of God are participants in the Eucharistic action. Jungmann's assertion, that this had been a feature of the primitive Eucharistic practice in Rome and had been gradually dissolved with the increasing clericalization of the liturgy the Middle Ages, has been shown to be wide of the mark. The primitive Roman liturgy was much more hierarchical, and less straightforwardly egalitarian in practice, than Jungmann and others have been prepared to admit (see Griffiths, 2012).[2] While other theological and ecclesiological factors might make the current practice of offertory processions highly desirable, it is quite another matter to claim that it is a rediscovery of long-lost ancient practice based on a debatable reading of the available historical evidence!

The Western 'ecumenical shape' of the Eucharist (typified by the Roman Catholic revision in the wake of the Second Vatican Council in the 1960s, and subsequent Anglican revisions such as *Common Worship*) have drawn heavily on data from the fourth century as a way of claiming a recovery of an authentic early practice (over and against insights and practices overlaid from the high Middle Ages). What cannot be ignored, however, is that the fourth century is the earliest period to provide contemporary liturgical scholars with data about the form and content of worship. Furthermore, this data was being interpreted at a time when the Church was seeking to respond to the decisive shift in political, social and cultural assumptions of the decades immediately following the Second World War. Might it have been the case that, with the benefit of hindsight, it is possible to detect that some evidence and data were selected to

---

2 The recent translation of *Ordo Romanus Primus* by Alan Griffiths (2012), with its detailed rubrics forming the basis of the text, demonstrates that the bread presented at the offertory at the Roman Mass in the eighth century was not only made by leading civic officials and other representative liturgical ministers, rather than 'ordinary' worshippers, but that it was not so much a case of these people *bringing their gifts to the altar* as the Pope and his liturgical *entourage coming down from the altar* to collect them from the Roman nobility. See also Bradshaw and Johnson (2012), pp. 204ff.

resonate with the cultural climate and expectations of the time? It is tempting ask to what degree the need to rebuild communities and nations after the devastating impact of ideological and military conflict, as well as the need to forge new political alliances, impacted on the prevailing theological, liturgical and ecclesial emphases invested in the reforms and revision of the Eucharist in the West in the second half of the twentieth century. Are the preponderant symbolism of the Church as the body as Christ, gathered around the Lord's table as the family of God, as well as the placing of altars in close relationship to the congregation and the emphasis on active vocal participation by all worshippers, as much a reflection of this impulse as of any renewed understanding of our Eucharistic origins?

Finally, any attempt to claim authenticity for a particular characteristic or practice in Christian worship, along with our attempts to interpret and apply it to our contemporary situation, requires attention to the insights informing L. P. Hartley's aphorism that 'the past is a foreign country: they do things differently there' (1953). That the pre-scientific Middle East in which early Christianity flourished and the oriental cultures into which it first spread were culturally, politically and theologically so unlike the world we currently know may seem overly obvious. However, it needs to be repeatedly stressed that how the Eucharist was understood and experienced, for example, by a North African worshipper in the mid-second century CE, living under absolute (and antagonistic) imperial power, without antibiotics, electricity, freedom of expression or choice, the ability to read or write or the capacity to travel very far from home and whose pace of life and manner of articulating 'truth' was quite unlike our own, presents a fundamental challenge to those who argue that texts and written evidence of liturgical practice from a specific period can tell us what worship was *actually like* then – and what it should be like *today*. Added to these obvious dimensions of 'unlikeness' must be the impossibility of imagining, in our own terms, how the Eucharist formed such worshippers in perceiving and relating to the ultimate unlikeness of God, at a time when Christianity was still in the process of becoming the largely settled, credal phenomenon we know today.

Having explored some of the historical issues which impinge on our understanding of the development of the Eucharist, what other factors might impact on a president's understanding of the origins of the Eucharist, its language and symbols, as well as the beliefs and practices which have informed its development – and which might inspire a renewal of contemporary practice?

This is a question worth asking in the light of the dominant assumption that the Passover–Synagogue model has been the prototype for our understanding of what has shaped the language, symbolism and ritual assumptions which underpin our Eucharistic origins. As I suggested in relation to the 'dual hypothesis' (see pp. 41–2), what follows is not so much an attempt to argue for the evolution of a separate and distinctive paradigm, but more of an attempt to redress an imbalance by highlighting influences which have not always been emphasized in recent liturgical, historical and biblical discourse. In short, I am suggesting that, alongside the accepted influence of Passover and synagogue, the language, symbolism and ritual assumptions of the Temple and the cult of sacrifice have also been undeniable impulses in the early development of the Eucharist.

Temple Altar or Kitchen Table?

The recent work of Margaret Barker has highlighted the degree to which, until relatively recently, it was largely assumed that the synagogue, not the Temple, was the singular source from which Christian worship sprang (see p. 44). Barker's broad argument is that, by looking at the New Testament (and post-biblical) evidence afresh, it is possible to reassess this previously unquestioned assumption. Barker's insights are supported by the work of others, such as Étienne Nodet (1998), who has observed the growing use of the language of sacrifice, influenced by Jewish Temple practice (and specifically the cult of the pre-exilic Temple) in Christian writings from locations outside Palestine, especially Rome and Antioch, towards the end of the first century CE. This strand of scholarly enquiry has highlighted a number of factors worthy of consideration.

First, although the language of the New Testament is clear that, as a consequence of the incarnation and resurrection of Christ and the sending of the Holy Spirit, there is no longer one designated place of divine encounter on earth (which was the function of the pre-exilic Temple and its Holy of Holies), and every place is, potentially, holy; it also continues to draw heavily on Temple imagery. It makes frequent reference to the first Christians worshipping in the Temple. It also points to the likelihood that the synagogue was an uneasy context for Christians by highlighting it as an arena for conflict between Jews and Christians; as well as being the place from which Christians were excluded. The language of high priesthood – a Temple ministry – was soon applied to the crucified and risen Jesus (e.g. Heb. 4.14). The post-Resurrection narrative in Luke as well as episodes in Acts place the worship of the first disciples and their followers in the Temple.

Barker further argues that the prophetic and ecstatic nature of the preaching of the disciples reflected a Temple rather than a synagogue tradition. The author of the book of Revelation identifies the Temple as the setting for the visions of heavenly worship; and, after its destruction in 70 CE, the language and imagery of the Temple persisted by being applied to Christians themselves. The author of the Letter to the Ephesians speaks of Christians as a 'living temple' (Eph. 2.19ff), and the author of the First Letter of Peter describes the Church as a 'royal priesthood' and as 'living stones' of a spiritual temple (1 Peter 2.5ff). Other similar examples suggest that Christians embodied the continuity of the Temple, with all its ethical as well as theological implications (e.g. Rom. 12.1; 1 Cor. 3.16, 16.19).

It is noteworthy, in these last examples, that Christian communities in Rome and Corinth, which are geographically and culturally distant from Jerusalem and the cult of the Temple, are exhorted and encouraged with language and imagery evoking its ritual assumptions. This can be explained, in part, by the presence of sizeable Jewish communities in Rome and Corinth which seem to predate any significant Christian presence, as well as the suggestion that diaspora Jewish communities maintained close links with Jerusalem and Palestine (Brown and Meier, 1983, pp. 95ff). There is evidence to suggest that Christian and Jewish communities in these and other cities were not especially isolated from other groups and that life in cities with large populations was a good deal more ethnically porous than might be supposed (Lampe, 2003, esp. pp. 19ff).

Second, account needs to be taken of the adoption of the language of priesthood and sacrifice in post-biblical literature, especially by the early years of the second century. As Barker has repeatedly emphasized, the Passover was the only Jewish ritual that did *not* require the ministry of a priest. Similarly, the covenant enacted at Passover was one of freedom from slavery and protection from plague (Exod. 12.12ff). The Passover originated as a domestic (and rural) ritual and only became part of the post-exilic Temple liturgy in Jerusalem. The language of the synoptic Gospel (and Pauline) accounts of the Last Supper do not immediately lend themselves to Passover themes, despite the close association with this festival in the positioning of the Gospel accounts of the Last Supper. The crucial point being that, in the Matthean account, the words spoken over the cup make reference to the 'new covenant in my blood' and 'the forgiveness of sins'. The Passover covenant is not sin-bearing; the covenant enacted on the Day of Atonement *is*.

Third, Barker argues that the translation of the words 'new covenant' spoken over the cup in the New Testament accounts of the Last Supper is problematic. For example, the earliest sources of the New Testament text do not contain the word 'new' (and some do not use it until as late as the fifth century). This presents the possibility that, for many people in the early Christian centuries 'the last supper was not about "the new covenant" but "*the* covenant"' [my italics]. Similarly, consideration needs to be given to what lies behind the Greek text of the New Testament. Matthew was a Jew writing for

Jews and, in Hebrew, the verb from which 'new' is derived is also used to mean renew (2008, p. 178). Consequently, it must be asked whether 'new' covenant was a recalling of an earlier Hebrew idiom; and that the inference was renewal and restoration of the covenant enacted on the Day of Atonement in the first Temple, known as the 'eternal' covenant first given at Sinai (Exod. 20).

Fourth, if the New Testament depicts the death of Jesus on the cross as renewing the eternal covenant, it is linked to the words of Jesus over the cup at the Last Supper. Significantly, it is the Jewish Matthew, writing for a Jewish audience, who would have been aware of several covenants in Judaism, who specifies that it is the covenant for the remission of sins. The Letter to the Hebrews explicitly compares the death of Jesus to the High Priest offering the sacrifice in the Temple on the Day of Atonement by entering the Holy of Holies with the blood that would be sprinkled in the Temple and to consume the bread of the presence. The liturgical practice of Temple required that the High Priest sprinkle the blood of the sacrifice, and in the Letter to the Hebrews this ritual act is linked to the shedding of Christ's blood on the cross (Heb. 10.19ff) along with the offering of incense to God who was enthroned between angelic attendants (Heb. 12.24ff).

The nature of the covenant enacted on the Day of Atonement was ultimately concerned with maintaining the *Sha'lom* between God and the whole created order. When this covenant was broken, the High Priest's sacrifice sought to heal the rupture and protect creation from the consequences of the breaking of the covenant by making atonement. This is the covenant specified in Matthew 26.28 (Barker, 2008, pp. 173–6).

Consequently, when account is taken of the earliest known Christian liturgies (e.g. the *Didache*), there is no suggestion of the Passover image of being liberated from slavery or protected from plague. Instead, there is thanksgiving for the gifts of knowledge and eternal life and for the name of God abiding in those who have received the bread and wine. This is wisdom imagery associated with the priesthood of the pre-exilic

Temple. The hope for the ingathering of the scattered Church into the Kingdom, which has become a text incorporated into many contemporary Eucharistic orders (including *Common Worship*),[3] is an image associated with covenant restoration on the Day of Atonement (Barker, 2008, p. 178).

Moreover, the writings of early, post-biblical figures (e.g. Justin Martyr and Origen) also interpreted the death of Christ in relation to the Day of Atonement, and this needs to be understood as much more than creative exegesis or straightforward allegory. Barker argues that the memory and handed-on mythology of the original meaning of the Day of Atonement as it was celebrated in the first Temple was influential in shaping the Eucharistic patterns of the first century of Christian witness. For example, Basil of Caesarea, when making reference to 'unwritten traditions' concerning certain liturgical rituals which are not endorsed by scripture (e.g. the invocation of the Holy Spirit over the bread and cup or turning East to pray), maintains that

> we are not satisfied with saying the words which the Apostle and the Gospel have recorded, but, before and after these words we add other words, on the grounds that they have great strength for the mystery. And these words we have received from the unwritten teaching. (*On the Holy Spirit* 66)

In a similar way, the use of the *Sanctus* in some early Eucharistic Prayers (from Isa. 6) evokes the Temple theophany at the burning of incense of the Day of Atonement; just as the human silence in the presence of the angelic attendants on God is made present in the Holy of Holies (cf. Hab. 2.20) and is recalled in the early Syrian anaphora of St James (a part of which has been

---

3 'As the grain once scattered in the fields and the grapes once dispersed on the hillside are now reunited on this table in bread and wine, so, Lord, may your whole Church soon be gathered together from the corners of the earth into your kingdom.' *Common Worship: Services and Prayers*, Holy Communion (p. 292).

popularized through Gerard Moultrie's metrication and translation in the hymn 'Let all mortal flesh keep silence').

Barker suggests the 'unwritten teaching' referred to by Basil is one source of evidence that certain rituals and traditions of the first Temple passed into the practice of the early Church (2008, pp. 212–13). For example, facing East to pray evokes the custom on the Feast of Tabernacles in the pre-exilic Temple (cf. Ezek. 8.16–18); and the invocation of the Spirit over the bread and wine is suggestive of the glory of the Lord being called down to fill the Temple (1 Kings 8.11), which points back to the calling down of the glory of the Lord to fill the Tabernacle (Exod. 40.34). Anointing with oil was a ritual practice found in the pre-exilic Temple, but not in its post-exilic successor. To apply the title 'Christ' (anointed one) to Jesus, and those who followed him as 'Christians' is deeply suggestive, alongside early Christian practice at baptism, particularly when account is taken of the ritual purpose of royal anointing in the first Temple to confer rebirth in the divine image (pp. 196, 212ff).

Fifth, the pre-exilic Temple was conceived as an embodiment of the whole cosmic order – both here and in eternity – and the veil of the Temple represented the frontier between the material world and the eternal sphere. Similarly, the Temple liturgy revolved around the maintaining of the eternal covenant, which held the cosmos together in peace; and, when broken, was restored by the high priesthood on the Day of Atonement. The pattern of its construction was linked to the pattern of creation in the first Genesis account. As Barker explains:

> The story of creation in Genesis 1 corresponded to the shape of the tabernacle or temple, and the formal assembly of the tabernacle, described in Exodus 40, shows that the stages of building corresponded to the six days of creation . . . Day One was understood to be the state of unity underlying the material creation . . . The second day was the firmament to separate heaven from earth, represented by the veil to separate the holy of holies from the great hall of the temple . . .

The sixth day was the creation of Adam, which corresponded to the consecration of the high priest. (2008, p. 11)

Temple and Church in Early Christian Consciousness

When the period of Christian persecution ended and buildings began to be adapted or built to house Christian worship, there are several reasons to suggest that Temple imagery was appropriated to describe them. Just as Margaret Barker has suggested that the Temple was understood as a microcosm of creation, and the sacrifice on the Day of Atonement was a means of restoring a broken creation, so early Christian reflection on the death and resurrection of Christ highlighted continuity between the shedding of Christ's blood and the renewal of creation. This is not only found in early Christian literature (e.g. Irenaeus, *Adversus Haereses* 5.19–21) but also in symbolic representation.

Stanislaw Chojnacki (2006) has drawn attention to the symbolism in the crosses of the Ethiopian Church, one of the earliest cultures in which Christianity took root outside Palestine, which depict the crucified Christ's blood streaming down a tree in full leaf to revive Adam, whose skull rests beneath it. Other crosses contain not only representations of leaves and palm branches, but also the birds of the air and the fish of the sea, with the suggestion that the cross gives renewed life to all creation.

J. G. Davies's influential study of church architecture (1968) alludes to the possibility that the demarcation of the sanctuary in the earliest Christian basilicas can be identified with the *penetralis* and *adytum* (the holiest places) of pagan temples, as well as identification with the Holy of Holies in the Jerusalem Temple. As Robin Gibbons has identified, such identifications gave rise to inherent tensions, with figures such as Hilary of Poitiers (d. *c.*368) and John Chrysostom (d. 407) challenging any automatic identification of the Church (as gathering of the holy people of God) with the church (as holy space). Nonetheless, there were texts which highlighted the connection between Solomon's Temple and the basilica in the late fourth century, when the notion of different 'zones' of varying degrees of sacredness began to be established. The place of the altar, where the intensity of the sacred was amplified by its being located over the tomb of martyr–saint, was the initial place to be figuratively identified with the Holy of Holies in Solomon's Temple. Subsequently, the baptistery, the nave and eventually the whole church complex, was invested with sacred meaning, as different areas were delineated. Certainly, by the sixth century, hymns written to celebrate the dedication of a church employ symbolic language to evoke the Temple and to emphasize the cosmic dimension of the church building as a holy place in which the liturgy celebrated the renewal of creation. This is expressed in the hymn used at the consecration of Hagia Sophia in Edessa:

> O Being Itself who dwells in the holy temple,
> whose glory [naturally] emanates from it
> grant me the grace of the Holy Spirit
> to speak about the temple that is at Urha . . .
> For it truly is a wonder that its smallness is like the wide world
> not is size but in type;
> like the sea waters surround it.
> Behold its ceiling is stretched out like the sky . . .
> And its lofty dome – behold, it resembles the highest heaven . . .
> Exalted are the mysteries of this Temple in which heaven and earth
> symbolise the most exalted Trinity and our Saviour's disposition . . .
>
> (translation by Kathleen McVey, 1983, pp. 91–121)

After Christianity became the privileged faith of the Roman Empire in 311/12 CE, and secular basilicas, with their rectangular and longitudinal shape, began to be adapted for Christian worship, their configuration was designed to draw the rshipper forward to where the liturgy, which celebrated the sacrifice of the cross, was celebrated at the far end. As Christopher Irvine (2013) has suggested, this placing of the liturgical action at the furthest point from where the building is entered was not so much to heighten the distance between worshipper and liturgical action as to provide a pathway along which a worshipper could approach the mysteries which celebrated the salvific restoring of a fallen creation and renewing the covenant of peace between God and humanity. Once churches began to be designed in cruciform shape, it is possible to see how they were invested with an added sacrificial and reconciling significance. Now, the building itself invited worshippers not only to look at and journey towards a liturgical enactment of the restoration of the cosmos; the building embodied it. In one sense, to enter the church building was to be spatially enveloped by the cross and the mysteries of salvation that are celebrated in the liturgy which takes place there. This is supremely expressed in the fact that many of those who designed and decorated the great Gothic cathedrals of European Christianity understood their task as much more than functional or aesthetic. The dimensions were often calculated with the cosmological and theological significance of the time, not least in relation to the flowering of Eucharistic devotion and theology. This can be understood as a reflection of what Margaret Barker has described as 'a blurring of the distinction between earth and heaven in the sacred space of the sanctuary' (1987, p. 240).

Re-Imagining Presidency in the Light of Historical Discovery

By sketching the brief – and selective – historical survey which is the theme of this chapter, I hope that contemporary presidents may sense that an awareness of history and, more specifically, an awareness of the complexity of the history of the evolution of the Eucharist, can inform, challenge and inspire a renewal and re-evaluation of Eucharistic presidency today. I want to suggest that a keener awareness of the tradition presidents inherit can impinge on the way they preside at the liturgy in several ways.

First, it may be that the Eucharistic president understands his or her role as much more than simply someone who models his or her ministry on the host at a domestic supper party, where a family or group of friends gather around the supper table, where there is a measure of friendship and intimacy, where all involved imagine that they are engaged in an uncomplicated recreation of what happened at the supper Jesus shared with his disciples on the night before he was crucified. The historical evidence I have highlighted suggests that, although the Last Supper provides the Church with a scriptural and archetypal warrant for the Eucharist, which may (along with other cultural conventions of eating and drinking) have informed the occasions of table fellowship which characterized early Christian identity, it cannot tell the whole story of how the Eucharist as we now know it has come into being. This is especially germane when consideration is given to the momentum which has accompanied the liturgical developments of the past half-century or so in the West. This has, generally speaking, tended to emphasize the Passover–Synagogue paradigm at the expense of the Temple–Sacrifice dimension. The model of the Church as the body of Christ has dominated our ecclesiological and liturgical assumptions, while other models of the Church (e.g. the pilgrim people, the prophetic herald, a communion of those seeking spiritual growth, a visible sacrament, as servants to the world, etc.) have tended to receive less consideration. This has fed an ecclesial and theological impulse which assumes that the task of the president is to nurture a gathered community around the table of the Lord, accompanied by liturgical assumptions which suggest that by privileging the (supposedly self-evident) practice of the fourth century, which had become distorted by the accretions of the high medieval period, it is possible to identify the essence of the Christian Eucharist. Our history is richer and its harvest for our understanding of the task of presidency infinitely more abundant. In a sense, presidency calls us to carry to the altar the accumulations of history which are not easily remembered, but which cannot so easily be dispensed with.

Second, if presidents are aware of the weight and fecundity of history, it may be that they begin to understand their ministry in broader terms: as also encompassing a sacrificial character, centred around Christ's atoning death and creation-renewing resurrection and as those who are called to draw worshippers into the mysteries of faith embodied and incarnated in the Church's sacrifice of praise. This may cause presidents to ask whether presiding at the Eucharist should seek to evoke theophany, of inviting worshippers into what Aidan Kavanagh famously called a 'liturgical seeing' (1990, pp. 255ff). This is about cultivating an awareness of the way in which the liturgy, as well as its physical setting and components, can become a context for apprehending the glory of God, of perceiving what is beyond the outward and physical dimensions of the worshipping environment and glimpsing the perspective of eternity which is foreshadowed in every Eucharist. The challenge implicit in such an understanding of presidency is that, if the Eucharist is much more than a 'supper' for a specific gathering of people, here and now, it must somehow be allowed to transfigure the disproportionately anthropocentric character it has come to acquire in recent decades. This calls for a particular sensitivity to the many ways in which worshippers may be enabled to get 'caught up' in the experience and environment of worship, in which their seeing, hearing and imagining are as much engaged as their speaking and singing. As Michael Sadgrove identified, such a perspective in liturgical presidency will invite those exercising this ministry to see that

[i]n the encounter with God which is worship, the sanctuary is charged with new perspectives on human life. We see what we could become. We see how the kingdom of God utterly transforms our 'take' on things. We see a new heaven and a new earth as if this world were already gathered up in the crucifixion and resurrection of Jesus Christ. (2008, p. 102)

Third, if a president's understanding of their ministry involves 'a blurring of the distinction between earth and heaven in the sacred space of the sanctuary' (Barker, 1987, see above, p. 60), considerable watchfulness should be exercised if the Eucharistic celebration and the environment in which it is celebrated is not to become inappropriately 'domesticated'. Sole reliance on the domestic character of the Passover archetype, coupled to a selective understanding of the Church as the body Christ (especially if it is deemed to be somehow equivalent to contemporary notions of 'family'), can give the impression of self-selection and even exclusivity. The prophetic description of the Temple as a 'house of prayer for all nations' (e.g. Isa. 56.7; Hag. 2.7) offers a necessary counterweight which echoes the Gospel parables of all sorts and conditions of humanity being invited to the banquet of the kingdom (e.g. Luke 14.20ff). It is the task of the president to widen the perspective of all who are being led in worship, to invite them to stand on the threshold of eternity as well as absorb the agony as well as the delight of the world, if the Eucharist is truly to be a foretaste of the eschatological banquet.

Similarly, when churches are excessively carpeted and cushioned or contain items more associated with the domestic kitchen or living room, it is often an outward sign of the cultivation of a congregational 'clubableness'. This can eclipse the president's more basic responsibility to open doors of perception on to the divine, as well signal cultural, historical and spiritual 'otherness' in the Eucharistic celebration. When more emphasis is placed on the notices and invitation to coffee than on the sermon or the Eucharistic Prayer, when the implicit invitation to gossip before worship is stronger than the summons to keep silence in the presence of God (often aided and abetted by the contemporary fascination with circular formation), there is more likely to be a confusion about the gravity of what is being celebrated in the Eucharist. This uncertainty is well-illustrated by an account I was once given of an early-morning Sunday Eucharist (according to the Book of Common Prayer) which began with the priest casually wandering into the place where it was to be celebrated and asking those gathered for worship: 'So who's not here this morning?' A more generous and inclusive perspective is effectively brought to bear if presidents possess a sufficiently confident grasp of the historical, theological and ecclesiological factors which inform their ministry. To preside at the Eucharist is, in a real sense, to stand in the gap between heaven and earth, past and present, local expectations and the exigencies of the whole human race, and to enact the sacrifice of praise which restores the peace between God and his fractured creation.

This chapter began with a quote from W. D. Davies, identifying an inherent tension in the beliefs and practices of the newly emerging Christian movement by probing whether the interdependence of land, Temple and Jerusalem, which are transfigured by Christ's death and resurrection, but also continued (and still continue) to shape Christian self-understanding. By drawing together the diverse historical threads of this chapter, it may not be unreasonable to suggest that something of this tension is both present and finds a measure of resolution, in the act of presiding at the Eucharist. It offers a framework of reflection which more than hints at the degree to which Eucharistic presidents need to be concerned with much more than a straightforward trajectory between contemporary relevance and unadulterated origins, but also need to embody an awareness of the multi-layered nature of the development of the words, symbols and actions which underpin the liturgy at which they preside. This is a way to embody both the host at supper and the priest in the temple.

3

Speech and Silence: The Possibilities and Limits of Language

Words strain
Crack and sometimes break, under the burden
Under the tension slip, slide, perish,
Decay with imprecision, will not stay in place,
Will not stay still.

('Burnt Norton', Eliot, 1944)

Ours is a culture which is impatient for clarity of meaning. The cultural momentum which has shaped the Western mentality over the past half millennium has favoured a mode of linguistic development in which the explicit and unequivocal is valued above the implicit, symbolic and metaphorical (see pp. 22ff). This poses a potential challenge to liturgical presidents, who are called to use words to enable a congregation to establish a relationship with a reality – God – who, experience and history has shown, eludes linguistic precision.

In liturgical celebration, a sense of divine reality is encompassed in poetry, symbol and metaphor, in space, colour, sound and silence. It is the task of the president to communicate this implicit meaning, not only through speech, but through gesture and music, by creating moments of intensity through silence and inhabiting space in a significant and representative manner. This immediately places the liturgical president in an uncomfortable place. Words of an implicit or symbolic quality are deeply counter-cultural. The Church's worship and mission is set in a context of 24/7 rolling news, where data can be obtained at the click of a mouse at any time of day or night, and information is provided in sound bites on demand.

The language of worship, by contrast, evolves slowly and its meaning is not instantly deciphered or defined. In a culture where written texts are largely disposable (and dispensable), while words rapidly proliferate through email and other social media, the language of worship requires us to wait: to be silent, to ponder and wrestle with the meaning and significance of speech which expresses praise and lament, elation and grief. As Avery Dulles (1994) has identified, there is an inherent tension between the language of worship and the language of a media-saturated society:

- The Church tends to mystery, the media to iconoclasm.
- The Church promotes eternal values, the media thrives on novelty.
- The Church strives for unity, the media seeks out conflict.
- The Church's values are spiritual, but the media is concerned mainly with its relationship to sex, politics and power.
- The Church is structured hierarchically, while the media favours the individual's right to autonomy and dissent.
- The Church's teaching is too subtle for journalists who require simple and striking stories.

Physical and Cultural

A cursory glance at the history of ideas similarly highlights the degree to which metaphorical and symbolic language (in poetry and philosophy in particular) has largely been subsumed, over the course of the past four centuries, by an appetite for the explicit. Clarity of expression is paramount. Neurological study is helpful in demonstrating how the momentum of recent history has helped to place greater emphasis on this cultural preference. The right hemisphere of the brain is concerned with absorbing not only new ideas and new encounters, but also our experience of the world, before the left hemisphere analyses and isolates that experience into rational and explicable categories. The right hemisphere of the brain delivers what Iain McGilchrist calls 'presences', before the left hemisphere re-appraises them and enables them to be sifted by referential language (2009, p. 179).

The primacy of the left hemisphere's preference for the explicit (which has become the mode by which most of our daily transactions are enacted in commerce, education, media, politics, etc.) is that it redefines what is new or unexpected and returns it as familiar and predictable. It transmutes what is unique (as seen, heard or felt for the first time) into the abstract and anticipated. By allowing the left hemisphere to dominate the right, language will lack spontaneity; and other implicit dimensions of life, such as a music, dance, humour, artistic creation or falling in love, become semi-artificial in the sense that the experience is diminished by analysis into 'what is already known' (2009, p. 180). The poetic and metaphorical nature of liturgical language, by contrast, differs fundamentally from the abstract and hypothetical. Instead, it opens up the possibility of depth, spontaneity and new discoveries:

Poets, and all makers of language . . . soar above the prevailing network of ideas in which our experience is confined . . . by ordinary language; they enable the rest of us to *see*, for the first time, in our own experience, something which may answer to these new and richer forms of expression, and by doing so they actually *extend* the scope of our *possible* self-awareness. They effect a real enlargement . . . and make new discoveries. (Scheler, 1954, cited in McGilchrist, 2009, p. 341)

This suggests that the language of liturgical celebration should invite, suggest, inspire and seek to open up new vistas. This is why the poetic, symbolic and metaphorical nature of liturgical language is a fundamental characteristic of the way Christians worship.

Unconventional Poetry

D. H. Lawrence (1929) described the poet as 'an enemy of convention'. In contrasting poetry with the language of everyday transaction, he esteems the poet as one who 'makes an untidy slit in the umbrella which humankind puts up to create a barrier between itself and the everlasting whirl' and opens up the conscience of those who are 'going bleached and stifled under their parasol'. Similarly, when the words of the liturgy are robbed of their potency, and the language of worship becomes 'stifled' by convention, it can contract, control and devalue the unseen and, as yet, unencountered possibilities which are integral to its 'unconventional' character.

This can be discerned in the poetry of Gerard Manley Hopkins, for example, whose work not only suggests a world shot through with the glory of God (what he called 'instress'), but does so through visual and aural perception rather than conventional verbal structures. Hopkins is a poet who used his eyes and allowed himself time and space to be encountered by the reality at the heart of objects and phenomena, rather than impose his own meaning or interpretation on them (what he called 'inscape'). Moreover, he reflected his discoveries back through the sounds and rhythms that his choice of words and the verbal stresses of his poems produced. Hopkins seems to have sensed that poetic language has its origins in music and dance, and in the spontaneous rhythms of breathing. He also knew that words can shrink the many-layered meaning of something as ordinary as a leaf by the control or restriction of meaning:

> Where we, even where we mean
> To mend her we end her,
> When we hew or delve:
> After-comers cannot guess the beauty been.
> ('Binsey Poplars', Hopkins, 1990)

When such considerations are brought to bear on liturgical language, and especially the words a president chooses to use (or not use) in the course of liturgical celebration, it becomes obvious that care must be taken to ensure that the language does not diminish or restrict what worshippers might potentially perceive – and receive. The perennial temptation is to collude with the current cultural demand for clarity of meaning in as short a time as possible, where deadlines loom, and targets drive the pace of life. Liturgical language, by contrast, should invite a slowing-down; create time to see and hear more than is possible at any one moment; and, above all, never attempt to short-cut the possibility of deeper discernment by resorting to the merely prosaic.

In a world where instant success (and gratification) is expected, the liturgical president is called to embody a different tempo and demonstrate that what is of enduring significance demands both time and heightened attention. Being called to minister in a world where language has become largely functional and mechanistic, the particular vocation of the liturgical president needs to be understood as one who uses words to encourage the thinking of new thoughts, to feel urgent hopes and to transfigure the superficial.

The Compulsion to 'Explain'

On holiday in a northern French city recently, I stumbled upon the centenary celebrations of the translation of the relics of the city's patron saint, which had been taken a century earlier from a Gothic city-centre abbey to a monastery about 20 km further along the valley. Much of the abbey's land and buildings had been given over to the state at that time and is now occupied by the *hôtel de ville* (town hall). The present monastic community had returned a century later to sing Vespers, at which the eponymous saint's present-day successor, the Archbishop, presided. There were over a thousand people in the church (most stood where they could), and the sense of excitement was palpable. A half-hour recital of organ and trumpet music seamlessly gave way to a characteristic 'French' improvisation on the abbey's renowned Cavaille-Coll organ, as the monks and their Abbot processed through the crowded church, followed by servers with incense, processional cross and lights, the secular clergy of the city and, finally, the Archbishop in cope and mitre with his retinue. It was a colourful and momentous spectacle. The organ music built up into a thundering crescendo as all the liturgical participants reached the Quire, and the climactic chord ended with resounding triumph. As the echoing organ music died away, there was an intense silence for about 15 seconds which felt as if it held everyone in the church on the precipice of expectation. The smaller organ, in the Quire, played the note for the cantor of the monastic choir to sing the opening words of the liturgy, *Deus in adjutorium meum intende* (O God, come to my aid). Instead of a lone human voice inaugurating the prayer of the Church, as it has done for centuries, with a musical motif older than Christianity itself, there was a noisy 'scrunch' over the sound system. The Archbishop invited everyone to sit down. For the next seven and a half minutes, he told us why we were there, what we would be doing and what 'graces' the liturgy would impart to those who participated in it. When this colourless, matter-of-fact digression had subsided, the congregation wearily rose to its feet; the organ once more played a note, and the liturgy recommenced as a single monk sang words and music that is part of his – and that of countless millions of Christians' – spiritual DNA. However, something vital had been lost in the intervening time, when that highly charged silence was fractured by the compulsion to 'explain'. Personalized words, which could not be remotely compared to the power of the music or the texts to which they were to be sung, undoubtedly reduced the experience and robbed it of its spontaneity and vigour.

There are many contexts where worshippers must endure the burden of the priest who believes it is not so much their task to preside at the Church's liturgy, but to explain it! They feel the urge to provide their own 'translation' of the words, their own interpretation of the actions and symbols, which has the potential to lessen its impact as an activity which is both distinctive and transformative.

The beginning of the Marriage liturgy often serves to illustrate this point. After the music, which has accompanied the bride and her father down the nave of a church, has subsided to coincide with that first nervous, but highly charged, glance between bride and groom, it often dovetails not into a hymn of praise or to the weighty words of the Church's liturgy, but to a cringe-worthy 'welcome' – complete with instructions about photography and confetti. Instead, the momentum of that walk down the church, accompanied by music and words of deep significance, should have been allowed to draw a couple into the mystery of the sacrament they will soon confer on each other. The momentum is irretrievably broken by the president's need to control the meaning and outcome of what is being experienced. This is a world away from Hopkins' sense of inscape, of allowing reality to emerge through patient attentiveness or making space for something to reveal its true self. As Kathleen Hughes has identified:

> We do not gather in the presence of the Holy One in order to discuss what we intend to do but to surrender to God's designs for us, a surrender that cannot be predetermined or controlled because it is not up to the initiative of the community. (1991, p. 71)

The American Roman Catholic scholar, Aidan Kavanagh, has addressed the tendency by presidents to turn the liturgy into what he calls a 'learning experience' by introducing the imaginary figure of Mrs Murphy (1992, pp. 145ff). Mrs Murphy is a lifelong worshipper, who is regularly exposed to the complex tapestry of activity which makes up the church's liturgy: not just its texts but its music, body language, colours, smells and tastes. Does she understand the real meaning of it all? In one sense, this is an irrelevant question for Kavanagh, who insists that Mrs Murphy is an implicit theologian. She may lack the vocabulary to articulate the meaning of what takes place in worship, but she experiences its power with no less reality or immediacy. By participating in the Eucharist and placing the prayers she says, the sins she confesses, the forgiveness she receives and countless other ways she senses the divine, a theological discourse is taking place. As Kavanagh has acknowledged elsewhere, liturgy 'deals not with the abolition of ambiguity but with the dark and hidden things of God. When it comes to liturgy, precision can be brought at too high a price, and some things cannot be said' (1982/90, p. 102).

Insecurity and Textual 'Tweaking'

Alongside the compulsion to explain, there seem to be many occasions where liturgical presidents feel the need to replace or supplement the words of the liturgy with their own. Although many examples of this behaviour can spring from a basic lack of self-awareness or failure to empathize adequately, much of it is rooted in far deeper anxieties and insecurities. Put simply, because too many presidents seem to lack a basic confidence in the capacity of the liturgy to communicate on its own terms, they project that insecurity on to other worshippers whom, they assume, are similarly uncertain, confused or bored by what is about to unfold. It appears as if a congregation cannot participate in the liturgy in any significant way unless it is specified, dissected and analysed beforehand.

By contrast, where there is a developed and nuanced self-confidence in the liturgy as a vehicle of revelation and an assurance in the president's own formation in the history and principles of the liturgy, it is possible to allow the liturgy to be, in R. S. Thomas's words, a 'laboratory of the spirit'. Where this confidence is eroded and cultural pressures to make it 'more accessible' are permitted to inundate a president's stance, the liturgy is in danger of promoting mutual insecurity between president and worshippers.

An anecdotal example of how this insecurity is often played out can be heard is in the manner of pronouncing the blessing at the conclusion of the liturgy ('and the blessing of God almighty . . . remain with you *always*'). These are words of considerable weight, which not only empower worshippers with the authority for mission, but also communicate an essential truth about God's bearing towards his people.

The all-encompassing adverb 'always', which is the climax of the blessing, is frequently qualified, redefined or explicated to a degree which suggests that the person pronouncing it is really quite unsure about its sufficiency or efficacy. Consequently, 'the blessing of God almighty' is invoked to remain with a congregation 'today, tonight, tomorrow, this coming week, in the days to come' and in countless other permutations which devitalize and desiccate the open-ended potential of the original. Similarly, 'remain with *you*' (plural in the Latin) is, again, frequently demarcated (and diminished) by being replaced with 'you, those you love, those you will meet . . .'. If the wind of the Spirit, to use the language of the Fourth Gospel, 'blows where it will', it at least suggests that liturgical presidents should possess sufficient confidence to believe and trust that the 'the blessing of God almighty' can be unleashed on the world without attempting to direct or control its impact!

Infantile Explanation?

Until relatively recently, it was almost de rigueur in many Roman Catholic churches for the formal liturgical greeting at the start of the Eucharist ('The Lord be with you . . .') to be immediately supplemented by 'Good morning, everybody', to which the congregation would dutifully respond 'Good morning, Father'.

This phenomenon begs fundamental questions about the significance of resorting to the lingua franca of the primary-school assembly and the impact it may be having on the nature of the relationship it implicitly (and explicitly) constitutes between president and people at the outset of the liturgy. Very often, it is rooted in a basic confusion about what makes liturgy distinctive and what place it occupies in the formation and growth of the people of God. If the president's fundamental assumption is that they are modelling the role of educated adult/teacher and that the congregation is the learning (or worse, uneducated) child/pupil, it is not only possible to detect a form of domination on the part of the president, who may be engendering tacit dependency by the congregation; it also highlights an implicit confusion about the interdependence of education and liturgy.

In Chapter 2, it was noted that, for the earliest generations of Christians, the liturgy had been a primary means of Christian formation (p. 48). The mystagogical approach of the early Christian centuries, which sought to enable new converts to inhabit the mysteries implicit in the Church's liturgical life, is comparable to 'inductive formation' in contemporary educational theory, where the subject under discussion is part of a person's lived experience before it is analysed or discussed. It is allowed to 'be' before it is examined in abstract. Account also needs to be taken of the fact that, historically, institutional Christianity emerged into a Graeco-Roman world in which education was concerned with the transformation of the whole person in a lifelong process. The *gymnasia* of the ancient world provided a rounded and integrated educational method from youth to adulthood, which was physical, mental and ethical. When Christianity emerged from persecution and was faced with the challenge of re-educating society, it absorbed the ideals of education in the Graeco-Roman world and sought to integrate all aspects of life into a pedagogy which promoted the transformation of the whole person. This educational model is concerned with much more than absorbing information, analysing texts in abstract or even prizing human knowledge as the final authority in discerning goodness, truth and beauty.

This gives some idea of how the overlap of liturgy and education has been significant throughout Christian history. As has been noted in relation to the current process of initiation in the Roman Catholic Church (p. 5), the liturgy has provided the basis for incorporating new converts into the sacramental life of the Church. Both then and now there is a clear perception that the liturgical rite can be experienced *as it is* with its many layers of visual, verbal, musical, symbolic and pictorial complexity.

However, such experience remains problematic for contemporary culture, and liturgical presidents who feel the pressure to speed up (or short-circuit) the time that this mode of formation requires need to recover a sense of confidence in the Church's deepest instincts about liturgy as an arena of education.

Kenneth Stevenson recognized this need for a much more nuanced interdependence of liturgy, education and spiritual growth, shortly after the publication of the *ASB*, where the drive for accessibility of meaning was becoming all-pervasive:

> we are in danger of neutering the whole exercise. Those who want the liturgy to be educational want to predetermine what the liturgy means and what it will teach the faithful . . . Educationally-minded presidents want to explain everything. I have witnessed the most excruciating liturgies when a well-intentioned priest has gabbled at such length about the 'meaning' of 'what we are about to do' that the symbolic act lay on the floor rather like pulped garlic . . . Education and growth are part of the liturgy, but to predetermine what is learned or to hasten how we are to grow inevitably means that the liturgy will snap, because it is approached by people whose expectations are too heavy and too specific. (1988, pp. 75–6)

Stevenson's concerns were voiced as Anglicans, Roman Catholics and members of the Free Churches were beginning to settle down to new patterns of revised worship which were characterized by 'contemporary' language. This process of liturgical revision had taken place in parallel with the drive for 'functional equivalence' in biblical translation (of which the *Good News Bible* is, perhaps, the iconic exemplar), building on the translational principles outlined by (among others) Eugene A. Nida and Charles R. Tabor (1969). A brief backward glance reveals an environment in which clarity of meaning was prized above rhythm, allusion, metaphor or tracing the poetic contours of texts. Readers were supposed to grasp not merely the translated text, but the translated *meaning* of the text, on first encounter.

A later generation of liturgists, notably many who have been involved in the *Common Worship* project, had recognized how texts need to be written with an underlying rhythm and with a view to being sung, where meaning is suggested, the imagination is triggered and the new and unexpected is anticipated. There has been a discernible move away from composing liturgical texts as step-by-step instruction manuals, to envisaging words as just one element in a multi-dimensional drama, where speech, action, music, silence, smell and colour communicate at different but equally valid levels.

Recognizing that liturgical language, however strange or even overwhelming, is nonetheless charged with meaning, raises a further challenge. This again relates to how texts are often subtly 'tweaked' or when there is such an indiscriminate use of alternative texts that the capacity to 'internalize' the liturgy is weakened. Words – especially liturgical or biblical words – can assume a sacramental quality. Their repetition is a necessary and vital component in allowing them to take hold of the imagination of worshippers and to shape their perceptions and expectations. To alter these words indiscriminately or to weaken their significance by providing a different 'version' of them each time they are spoken is a serious mishandling of the Church's collective prayer, and potentially deprives worshippers of one of the means of divine self-disclosure.

Imposition?

Stephen Sykes has written of this tendency to tweak and replace. He described it in terms of an 'alien imposition'. Recognizing the contemporary consumerist preference for endless variety and a sense of cultural boredom at frequent repetition, he suggests that liturgy locates worshippers in a specific social space, constructs the horizons of their world, prompting to (or dissuading from) certain courses of action. It is, he argues, an archetypal model of domination – particularly so because of the way words (and the choice of those words) are spoken into such an arena, because of who is authorized to speak them and, more significantly, to change them. To repeat certain words and phrases enables them to be interiorized through memory; and, because memory is a function of the brain, what is committed to memory is physically 'within us' and can be as sacramental in quality as the bread eaten and the wine drunk at the Eucharist.

> The nervous flitting from text to text, which sometimes goes under the euphemistic heading of 'enrichment', is an all-too-faithful reflection of the superficiality of our culture and its obsessive fear of boredom. (Sykes, in Brown and Loades, 1996, p. 162)

As I was approaching my ordination as a priest, I was encouraged, as part of my daily discipline over several months, to learn particular texts of the Eucharistic rite by heart (the Greeting, Collect for Purity, Absolution, Offertory Prayers, Invitation to Communion, Blessing, etc.) and also to absorb something of the underlying principles informing the texts which might change seasonally (invitation to the general confession, the verses that are interpolated with the *Kyrie eleison* as an alternative to the general confession, the introduction to the Peace, etc.). It proved to be a liberating exercise, because it not only relieved me of the burden of being visually absorbed in the printed text, it also released me to concentrate my energy on appropriate body language and gesture (see Chapter 4). It also allowed for a measure of the unforeseen and unexpected in the way the words were spoken and heard in different circumstances. Significantly, it ensured that, on those occasions when a text was missing, I either had some recall from memory or was able to improvise with a degree of faithfulness to the principles of the original without sacrificing the integrity of the liturgy.

The integrity of the liturgical text is, of course, crucial for Anglicans, for reasons already outlined (see p. xi), precisely because it articulates the foundational *kerygma* of the Gospel. In other words, the liturgy needs to be a faithful reflection of received revelation, where the words and metaphors of the

Gospel are allowed to speak on their own terms, because worship is a response to the God who is revealed through the proclamation of the Gospel. Where the received liturgy is arbitrarily altered, and metaphors are translated into something deemed more 'accessible', there is always the possibility that something essential may be compromised. As David Brown has recognized, 'The Bible must in some sense be allowed to speak for itself. Otherwise, it is another gospel that is being proclaimed' (2008, p. 115).

A further insight is offered by Catherine Pickstock, whose predilection for the medieval forms of the Mass may be considered over-romantic, but who nonetheless maintains that the value of repetition in an imperfect, earthly liturgy could be considered as *rehearsal* for the perfect worship of eternity. In her consideration of the 'Impossibility Liturgy' (1998, pp. 169ff) she identifies the verbal and supplicatory repetitions of the Medieval and Counter-Reformation Mass, along with its 'stops and starts', to propose that worshippers need to use liturgical language repetitively as a way of entering and re-entering into the presence of God. When the words of the liturgy are 'rehearsed' through repetition it is done 'in the hope that there might be worship' (p. 200). This was echoed by David Frost, who has composed some of the most resonant liturgical texts currently in use in the Church of England:

> If liturgy is to justify its existence, its language must be such that minister and people can return to it again and again and discover further meanings at each repetition: it must have rhythm, imagery and verbal punch such as can only be achieved by leaving yourself a wide variety of ways in which to say something: in other words, it needs something of the quality of poetry. For this reason the churches have commonly drawn material from Scripture, which has this richness and density of meaning. (1973)

Such insights demonstrate the degree to which liturgical language probes the depths of human encounter with the divine. It can touch the most tender of human nerves because language, employed as a means of signalling the dissimilarity between worship and other human activity, can easily feed a perception that liturgical celebration is merely about preserving archaisms for reasons of cultural polity. Consequently, the dimension of difference or otherness becomes obscured by an underlying antipathy which can repel as well as invite.

This is a topic which, at the time of writing, is exercising many English-speaking Roman Catholics, who are coming to terms with a new translation of the liturgy. The Latin text has been deliberately translated to reflect the syntax and sentence construction of the original language. This departure from 'functional equivalence' towards a more literal rendering of the text has introduced a linguistic component which provides the repetitive dimension that Pickstock and others have suggested is missing from more recent liturgical compositions.

The overall result is a style of sacral language which is quite unlike the natural speech patterns of everyday life – formal, informal or intimate – and it seems to be a bold assumption that a single translation will uniformly serve all English-speaking cultures. The very strangeness of the language (epitomized, perhaps, by the change from 'and also with you' to 'and with your spirit' in response to presidential greetings) and the literal manner in which the Latin liturgical text is preferred over scriptural resonances (most notably in the use of the word 'chalice' for 'cup' at the institution narrative and other places in the Eucharistic Prayers). The supplicatory, even pleading, character of the Latin original is as arresting as it is challenging – not least for those who preside. A significant number of the Collects, for example, call for a marked degree of breath control in order to keep the subject of the verb in focus:

As we receive the pledge of things yet hidden in heaven
and are nourished while still on earth
with the Bread that comes from on high,
we humbly entreat you, O Lord,

that what is being brought about in us in mystery
may come to true completion.
Through Jesus Christ . . .

> (Post-Communion Collect for Third Sunday of Lent,
> Roman Missal, 3rd edn, 2011)

It is significant that, alongside a welcome from those who
believe that earlier translations had been an inadequate reflection of the original, questions of 'alien imposition' (see above,
p. 76) have also been to the fore in the reaction to this
most recent translation,[1] and a significant elapse of time will
be required to judge whether this mode of liturgical language,
which not only departs from the grammatical patterns of contemporary spoken English, but also from several decades of
shared ecumenical use, will, in T. S. Eliot's words, 'reach /Into
the silence'. For, as the poet observed, 'Only by the form, the
pattern, / Can words or music reach / The stillness . . .' ('Burnt
Norton', 1944).

Improvisation

Earlier, account was taken of the interrelatedness of oral culture
and faithfulness to tradition, particularly in the Middle Eastern
cultures from which Christianity first emerged (see p. 46).
This becomes significant when considering the question of how
a president's choice of words might amplify (or reduce) the
potential for a congregation to 'hear the Gospel' – especially
when resorting to improvisation. A superficial understanding
of improvisation assumes an absence of structure and form,
something uniquely 'made up' on the spur of the moment,
which bears little or no relation to what has gone before: a
uniquely individual and unrepeatable creation.

---

1 See the Liturgical Texts Debate within the Irish Association of
Catholic Priests: www.associationofcatholicpriests.ie/category/liturgical-
texts-debate/.

However, this is a mistaken description of an improvised art-form; and, if taken too seriously, will result in little more than repetitive meandering. By contrast, effective musical improvisation, if it is to have any artistic integrity, is far more dependent on tradition and form, where thematic and stylistic cohesion are necessary components. Musical improvisation, whether in jazz or in more 'classical' idioms, usually happens after sustained exposure to a musical genre and repeated experimentation (usually in private) before it is performed in the public arena. Consequently, accomplished musical improvisers have gained a level of technical competence, as well a reasonable grasp of musical theory. They will also have cultivated some sensitivity towards the conventions of stylistic development and a willing-ness to empathize with the creative impetus which gave rise to the themes and ideas which form the basis of an improvisation. As one leading exponent of organ improvisation has acknow-ledged, many children who begin to learn an instrument often find that, in parallel with learning composed pieces, they engage in a form of 'aural research' by creating sound patterns (espe-cially on the keyboard) and that this is a positive means of both stimulating musicality *and* absorbing the essential characteris-tics of a particular musical language (Briggs, 2010). However, it does not happen in a vacuum, and is undertaken in relation to a received musical 'canon'. For example, Frederick Chopin (1810–49) was renowned, from an early age, for being able to improvise to perfection in the style of his predecessors J. S. Bach (1685–1750) and Mozart (1765–91), which is said to have informed his own distinctive compositional voice.

In her work on biblical interpretation, Frances Young uses the analogy of musical improvisation and in particular the cadenza to illustrate how scriptural texts might be 'performed' in Chris-tian worship. Recognizing that the cadenza is the moment in a musical work (usually a concerto) when the soloist is given an opportunity to 'break free' of the orchestra and the score, to offer a display of improvised brilliance, Young also acknowledges that this improvisatory form never takes place in creative isolation. Rather, there is an inherent tension in the need for freshness and spontaneity coupled to an awareness of the intentions of the composer. Soloists cannot improvise a cadenza to a concerto by Mozart, for example, if they have no grasp of the essence of Mozart's compositional intentions. A true cadenza is enacted when the original score and the immediate context interact:

> It must be integrated with the 'given' score, through a development of it, and it must engage others in the unity of the whole. On the one hand, the soloist is able to produce a show of skill, and without the performer's total involvement – indeed projection of her personality – the cadenza would be dull and uncommunicative. On the other hand, the soloist is the servant of the music – bringing out what is potentially there in the themes and harmonies of the original score. If that is not the case, the cadenza will not 'belong' to the performance of this particular classic. (1990, p. 161)

What is true of music is equally true of words, and those who seek to improvise from scriptural or liturgical texts need to discover how to restate the themes anew with creative integrity. An awareness of contemporary need and the demands of the immediate context will be informed by philological skills, hermeneutical insights and an imagination that is fed by sustained reflection on the text and its use in the overall momentum of Christian tradition. The challenge is to discern how improvisatory language is not completely alien to the liturgy which surrounds it.

This reflects insights from human development, where language is learned by imitation from an early age. What we suppose is expressed freely and unconsciously, is, in fact, absorbed through a complex process of hearing, copying, empathy, impersonation, as well as intuition. Unless account is taken of how words are used or sentences structured, communication becomes impossible, and the result is an unfocused confusion of sounds. However natural our ability to express ourselves through speech may seem, it is the outcome of a consistent exposure to structures, principles and conventions formed by others and subject to evolution, throughout the course of history.

Such factors are often ignored when it comes to liturgical improvisation, to the extent that those who resort to it as a preferred medium for leading worship often deliver a more ritualized and inhibited vocabulary than those who rely on an authorized and commonly recognized liturgy. The repetition of the same phrases and words becomes stale and clichéd; and (as I know from personal experience of resorting to improvisation when leading the Prayers of Intercession, for example, at the daily Eucharist) without preparation and reflection, the boundaries of so-called freedom are easily reached and exhausted. Moreover, the outcome is often a sort of linguistic 'splashing around in the shallow end of the pool', where it becomes apparent that what is being spoken is inadequate. This provokes a seemingly endless grasping for the right – and satisfying – words or phrases. Put simply, those who improvise without form and structure, without sustained exposure to the tradition, without sensitivity to the development of liturgical language and the instincts of the Church as a whole, will find it difficult to know when to stop talking!

When I moved from parish ministry to the more liturgically discriminating world of a cathedral, I was required to lead the Prayers of Intercession at Evensong several times each week. At first, I resorted to improvising an introduction to each of the collect-style prayers after the anthem (e.g. 'Let us pray for the world in all its trauma and heartache . . .'). After only a few weeks it became painfully apparent that I was hearing the reverberation (literally!) of my own stock phrases to such an extent that it became unsustainable. The element of immediacy and originality had quickly been eclipsed by a jaded predictability. What had been bearable once a fortnight in a parish church could not stand more frequent repetition on a daily basis in a place where the sweep of the musical, liturgical and architectural history surrounding my words demanded something more rigorous and enduring.

The resolution lay in a more disciplined approach: by paying attention to the words and images of scripture, to the writings of significant personalities in Christian history, to the form and content of the liturgy (in other traditions as well as my own) and to the work of contemporary writers who seemed to exemplify good practice. More crucially, I recognized that, in order to convey a sense of spontaneity, these introductions would need to be scripted – precisely in order to edit out the repetitive clichés and 'splashing around'. Even so, when pushed for time or tired, it was always possible to lapse – as I discovered when a colleague, walking home with me after Evensong one day, asked, 'How was God's broken but beloved world for you today?'!

Peter Brook has identified how, in the arena of theatrical production, the aim of improvisation is to get away from what he calls 'Deadly Theatre'. He describes a theatrical exercise which is aimed at repeatedly bringing actors to their own barriers and to the point where, in place of new-found truth, improvisation normally substitutes a lie. An actor playing a scene falsely by superimposing his own interpretation of a character or substituting his own words appears false to the audience because 'he is substituting false ideals for real ones: tiny transitional phoney emotions through the imitation of attitudes'. Therefore, the purpose of the exercise is to 'reduce and return: to narrow the area down and down until the birth of a lie is revealed and caught. If the actor can find and see this moment he can perhaps open himself to a deeper, more creative impulse' (1968, pp. 112–13).

Something of this dynamic is at play in the way scripture is used to underpin the improvisatory nature of worship in the Free Churches. Traditionally, the minister is given considerable freedom, within a broad framework, to use words of their own choosing to clothe the liturgical skeleton. The opening prayer in Free Church worship, for example, is characteristically improvisatory in nature (if not in reality), and will usually encompass exaltation and worship, penitence, thanksgiving and petition. It is a liturgical form akin to a musical cadenza (see above, p. 82), in which the language and imagery of scripture is expressed with originality in a moment of focused attentiveness within the overall flow of worship. However, the best examples are manifestly the outcome of a prolonged wrestling with scripture and tradition, of searching for language and images which are faithful to revelation. It was memorably expressed by the Baptist liturgical scholar, Neville Clark:

> Scripture exists for the sake of proclamation . . . It is a Word once spoken that clamours to be spoken again, a story once told that presses towards retelling . . . Even at its most theological and conceptual, it is restlessly pushing back towards the patterns of oral speech, address and conversation, intent on recreating the immediacy of face-to-face encounter. The preacher . . . is forced to enter into linguistic travail. The Word must find words. (1991, p. 90)

This suggests something far more than simply replicating the syntax of the original or striving for an authentic rendering of a text (even in translation), because no liturgical president ever speaks words into an entirely neutral arena. Rather, by improvising from scripture and tradition, the essential task is to discover the means to express the salvific and revelatory character of the original in such a way that it becomes discernible in the present and opens up tantalizing possibilities for the future. It invites the liturgical president to choose language that allows texts once proclaimed in different historical and cultural circumstances to be spoken with a ring of authenticity into the exigencies of today – and tomorrow.

The Weight of Words

The satirical portrayal of the vicar with the 'plummy' voice, the stock-in-trade of 1970s television comedy, may be a thing of the past. The opposite tendency is now more likely to prevail, where a desire for 'personal authenticity' causes many liturgical presidents to play down the representative nature of their role – especially in the way they 'perform' the text of the liturgy and use their voice. This gives rise, in some circles, to the suggestion that presidents should 'read it like the telephone directory' and avoid all emphasis or nuanced use of the voice. While presidents should resolutely eschew the adoption of a liturgical *persona* which might eclipse their true selves, they cannot avoid the reality that they are called to embody a *representative* character (see p. 32). This is vital if a president is to avoid conveying the impression that what is being spoken in the liturgy is of little significance or that the words have no power beyond themselves to open up other vistas. Rather, the imperative must be a desire and a capacity to 'embody' through speech the mysteries at the heart of the Church.

Peter Brook has identified the dangers inherent in both a mechanical delivery and in an over-affected liturgical demeanour. What he called 'Deadly Theatre' can appeal to nostalgia or becomes an unconvincing compromise which is neither everyday speech nor over-dramatic declamation:

> A word does not start as a word – it is an end product which begins as an impulse, stimulated by attitude and behaviour which dictate the need for expression. This process occurs inside the dramatist; it is repeated inside the actor. Both may be conscious of the words, but both for the author and then for the actor the word is a small visible proportion of a gigantic unseen formation. Some writers attempt to nail down their meaning and intentions in stage directions and explanations, yet we cannot help being struck by the fact that the best dramatists explain themselves the least. (1968, pp. 12–13)

This suggests that good liturgical presidency is not simply a matter of one-dimensional communication, of reading the text in a particular and presupposed manner. Clear account needs to be taken of the way in which president and the congregation are engaged in a two-way communication, not just through verbal participation such as spoken responses etc., but also in the largely unspoken expectations and experiences they bring with them to the arena of worship. Added to this is the further dimension of divine communication in the liturgy: of God's own self-disclosure and also of giving expression to how the congregation is caught up in Christ's own self-offering to the Father.

An illustration of what this might mean in practice is offered by Peter Brook's description of the Royal Shakespeare Company's 1964 European tour of *King Lear*. He recalls how the best performances occurred between Budapest and Moscow. In these locations, audiences were made up of people who had very little knowledge of English, yet they had a profound influence on the cast. They came to each performance with a love of the play itself; with a real hunger for contact with foreigners from the 'free' world and an experience of life on the far side of the Iron Curtain that enabled them to relate directly and personally to the play's painful themes of justice and brutality, authority and chaos, wisdom, madness (especially as it relates to those in authority) and betrayal.

> The quality of the attention that this audience brought expressed itself in silence and concentration; a feeling in the house that affected the actors as though a brilliant light were turned on their work. As a result the most obscure passages were illuminated; they were played with a complexity of meaning and a fine use of the English language that few of the audience could literally follow, but which all could sense. (1968, p. 22)

In contrast to this experience, Brook recounts how the tour then moved to the United States, where the audience could understand the English language perfectly well, but simply did not engage with the play's themes and sub-texts in the same way. The stressed themes, which were vivid and immediate to the people of the (then) Eastern bloc, were not relevant to an educated middle-class living in a free-market society. The quality of the acting had deteriorated – precisely because the cast's relationship with the audience had changed. The actors soon sensed this, and the stresses changed by underlining everything in the play that would arrest audiences in a new situation, by giving less emphasis to the intricate passages that the non-English audience had so enjoyed.

Relational Language

In the celebration of the liturgy there is a similar meeting of experience, as worshipper and Christian tradition are brought into direct relationship, where the president seeks to invite a discovery of the Other. In the prevailing Western cultural context, where words (and verbal texts in general) are regarded as isolated and cerebral, as merely ink on paper, it highlights the potential for the effective speaking of words in a dramatic context, where their capacity to transform is heightened because they are set in dynamic relationship to space, music, gesture, symbol – and a body of worshippers which experiences these things in relation to their wider cultural surroundings. Words, especially liturgical words, should expand (not restrict) meaning and invite those who encounter them into a world awaiting exploration – even where their meaning is not immediately obvious.

David Brown has suggested that, when words are isolated from the human voice and afforded a quasi-factual status, there always exists the potential for them to become idolatrous (2008, esp. pp. 131ff). Language, like art, achieves its effect not by tightly defining reality, but by inviting exploration. When words are spoken they take on a provisional and open-ended character. What, at first, seems uncertain can lead, in time, to the discovery of the transcendent and complete.

The Limiting Impact of Technology

Such an insight offers both opportunity and challenge to the liturgical president because the development of modern technology (beginning with the invention of the printing press), which is often hailed as a liberating force for language and literacy generally, also had contrary (and restraining) consequences. It has been suggested, for example, that the invention of the printing press contributed to the fossilization of Roman Catholic liturgy for four centuries, because it had the effect of making texts (and forms) 'standard'. Having the

Counter-Reformation liturgy fixed in printed form, coupled to universal distribution from a central 'authority', removed the possibility of the local diversity and distinctiveness which had been a feature of earlier, pre-Reformation medieval patterns.

Similarly, the advent of computerized liturgy, which has been designed to encourage local creativity and diversity, has also had the effect of what Susan White calls the 'bureaucratization' of worship (1994). This is what happens, for example, when a 'local elite' decides what the textual form of the worship will be, and the shape and momentum of the liturgy is conceived purely in terms of texts on paper. This is frequently observed in the contemporary Church of England, where the scope of textual variety offered by *Common Worship* and the availability of those texts in electronic form have not only encouraged a culture where all emphasis is determined solely by textual variation; it has limited the potential for that emphasis to evolve or develop because the written text establishes what the liturgy will be. Ironically, technology then becomes a means of resisting, rather than enabling, change and development.

This has resulted in a measure of 'textual overload' at key moments in the liturgical year because too much is being demanded of textual variety and textual additions in order to make the liturgy distinctive. Not surprisingly, the actual 'feel' of the liturgy remains static because, apart from different words on paper, nothing of the spatial, visual or symbolic dimension of the worship has changed. Distinctive texts, unless they are 'received' differently, will not necessarily make the overall impact of the liturgy distinctive.

Words and their Context

When Michael was inducted into his new parish in mid-October, he soon realized he should discover how the worshipping community in that place would celebrate the liturgy in Advent. He was enthusiastically told that the parish had its own specially devised booklet with the 'Advent version' of the Parish Eucharist (using *Common Worship*, Holy Communion, Order One and material from *Times and Seasons*) and that it had been carefully devised to mark the season out from other times of the year. When Michael saw this booklet, he realized that it was almost identical in shape to the 'Lent' version of the parish's Sunday Eucharist. He also recognized that what made Advent distinctive in that community was a different form of the general confession, a different affirmation of faith to replace the Nicene Creed and a different versicle and response to the Prayers of Intercession. He also saw there was a seasonal introduction to the Peace, Prayer of Preparation of the Table and introduction to the Lord's Prayer. There was also a different form of words to accompany the breaking of the bread and the invitation to communion. At the conclusion of the service, just before the blessing, there was a series of acclamations (a dialogue between president and congregation) using a seasonally appropriate collage of biblical texts. After looking through the booklet, he asked the musicians, servers and people who exercised a ministry of welcome, how they 'did' the service. 'Just as we always do' they replied!

The following year, Michael met with the ministry team, musicians, servers and others and explored how words, music, movement, space and overall mood might enable the liturgy in Advent to be distinctive. The group was encouraged to suggest, by thinking about the building, their musical resources and the symbols they could use, how worshippers might enter into an experience of joyful expectation and reflect on the traditional themes of Advent, with their emphasis on death, judgement, heaven and hell. Having considered the 'environment' in which the liturgy would be celebrated and into which words would be spoken and sung, they looked at specific texts. The key elements of the liturgy were:

- **Colour:** A decision was made to use blue rather than violet for Advent. This had been the traditional English custom before the Reformation. It helped to distinguish Advent from Lent and invited reflection on the juxtaposition of hope, joy and judgement which makes Advent different from the explicitly penitential season of Lent.
- **Symbol:** Previously, the Advent Wreath had been lit before the Eucharist began, with one of the children from the Sunday School being called out to light the next candle just after the president had given an informal welcome before the opening hymn was sung. Now, the lighting of the Advent Wreath was incorporated into the introductory rite of the Eucharist with appropriate music, movement and spoken acclamations after the greeting.
- **Movement:** Their church was a large, spacious building, with the worship space located, more or less, in the middle of the building with more space beyond it to the 'East'. It was decided that the opening procession would not move from 'West to East' (from the back of the church towards the worship space) as it usually did, but would begin far away at the East end of the church. It would also involve fewer ministers (just the president, assisting ministers and servers) along with a young member of the congregation, clearly visible and carrying a lighted taper which would be used to light the Advent Wreath. The intention was to create a sense of waiting for the light to arrive from a distance, accompanied by music not heard at any other time of the year, in which the congregation was given a short 'refrain' to sing at the end of longer verses sung by the choir alone. This heightened the sense of waiting and expectation.
- **Shape and length:** It was felt that, because Advent was a season of preparation, it might be appropriate to 'fast' from certain elements of the full liturgical provision and allow people to experience a contrast when the festivities of Christmas arrived. Consequently, the opening of the service was 'paired down'; there was more use of silence; some hymns

were differently positioned in the liturgy from usual. As one of the group suggested, with an allusion to John the Baptist as a central figure in the Advent narrative, 'When you're waiting in the desert, you have to make do with less.'

- **Texts:** Only after the questions of colour, symbol, movement and shape had been considered did the group think about what texts might highlight these emphases. Significantly, much of the discussion was focused on which texts might *not* be used, as well as looking at seasonally distinctive possibilities.

Words in a Pictorial World

This chapter began by acknowledging that the world we inhabit and the language we encounter strives for the explicit. The media-saturated world which shapes most peoples' expectations is suspicious of language that seems to invite further scrutiny instead of providing immediate clarification. This is precisely why most journalists are impatient with much church-related discourse, because it requires them to take account of a wider cultural and historical context. It reduces the potential for presenting an issue in a pacey style, easily presentable to the non-specialist, which allows for an eye-catching headline. Paradoxically, the same media-saturated world relies increasingly on the pictorial and iconic to communicate ideas simply and strikingly through televisual and information technology; which means that televisions, computers and telephones have overtaken even tabloid newspapers as the preferred medium of communication for a significant section of the population of the Northern hemisphere – notably among those socio-economic groups with whom the Church of England has not easily connected through its formal worship. This use of pictorial images, coupled to the promotion of the cult of celebrity, is content with the superficial and impatient with the need to give attention to deeper meaning, or to allow images and icons to challenge values and perceptions. The expansion of social networking, such as Twitter, has stretched this demand for ideas to be communicated as clearly as possible in as few words as possible. As R. S. Thomas identified in one of his last poems:

> Vocabulary is no longer the ladder
> Angels ascend and descend
> On. It is flashed at us
> Too rapidly for us to cherish.
> It is thrown away
> When it no longer earns its keep
> As an advertiser.
>
> ('The greatest language . . .', Thomas, 2002)

The liturgical president is challenged to pay close attention to such developments – not least in crafting words which evoke images and experiences. This is a stock-in-trade for those who frequently broadcast through the medium of radio, for example. Of equal importance is the need to impregnate liturgical language with a sense of rhythm which stimulates the imagination and enables words and phrases to become lodged in the individual and collective memory. For some presidents, this will require an element of 'unlearning' some unhelpful linguistic developments which characterized the decades leading to the publication of the *Alternative Service Book*. With a drive for clarity of meaning, there was also a reliance on concepts. This was often highlighted (as much by poets and musicians as by popular satire) in contrast to the rhythmic and pictorial elements of the Book of Common Prayer. This contrast can be clearly discerned in the forms of General Confession:

> we have erred and strayed from thy ways like lost sheep:
> We have followed too much the devices and desires of our own hearts . . .
>
> (BCP, Daily Office: Morning Prayer)

> we have sinned against you
> and against our neighbour
> in thought and word and deed,

through negligence, through weakness,
through our own deliberate fault.
(*ASB/CW*, Confession from Holy
Communion, Order One)

The first example could be easily dismissed as an archaism
from a long-forgotten agrarian society; except that it evokes
an experience and invites a measure of visualization which the
latter example does not. This is a dimension which *Common
Worship* deliberately attempted to address and is especially
present in the 'Additional Collects', for example:

In the depths of our isolation
we cry to you, Lord God:
give light in our darkness
and bring us out of the prison of our despair;
through Jesus Christ our Lord.
(*CW*, Additional Collects, Easter Eve)

A similar approach can be found in Alan Griffiths' (2004) translation of the collects from the Ambrosian Sacramentary, which
are crafted (and translated) in language which more vividly
echoes the language and images in the day's scriptural readings;
as well as in the prayers which follow the Psalms in *Common
Worship Daily Prayer*, as an alternative to the *Gloria Patri*.

This dimension seems especially lacking in texts which are spoken in the 'gathering' moments of the liturgy – whether improvised or using the set form. It is rare to hear language which
invites and enables a longed-for catharsis in the act of confession, for example, where the conceptual and 'generally speaking'
complexion of a text lacks any depth of emotional intensity:

Let us confess our sins in penitence and faith,
firmly resolved to keep God's commandments,
and to live in love and peace with all.
(*CW*, Prayer of Penitence, Holy Communion,
Order One)

A heightened sensitivity to the way language (and the rhythm of words) can make this moment of attentiveness more vivid might employ a different linguistic pallet:

> For the words we have spoken,
> for the choices we have made for our own advantage
> which cause others hurt, even now,
> let us implore the mercy of God.

The language of invitation to confession might also set the abundance of God's mercy in proper relationship to an awareness of the gravity of individual and corporate sin:

> When fears deep within provoke us to words of hatred and hostility;
> when our silence at the plight of the hungry and the homeless adds to the weight of their suffering and indignity;
> we open our hearts once more the immensity of God's mercy
> which is infinitely greater than our failure to love our neighbour.

Much has already been written elsewhere about Prayers of Intercession which lack passion and engagement.[2] Again, there is a delicate balancing act to be achieved between a drive for perpetual novelty and a degree of predictable repetitiveness which blunts worshippers' receptivity to this focused moment of the liturgy. Paul Iles has written of the subtle balance of words

---

2 Green (1987) suggests that 'Intercession is the work of co-creation ... the focus around which we build our defences against doubt ... The lectures to God that we hear so often at this stage of the Eucharist are little more than a sign of deep mistrust. I shall never forget the three-minute obituary notice that God heard on the Sunday after Joyce Grenfell's death – God does not need to be told all the facts! Intercession can be a means of enlarging the fantasy that we can control God ... at its best [it] is our affirming the good purposes of God in the whole universe, even if they cannot be fathomed' (p. 43).

and silence, action and stillness, public and personal aspiration which undergirds the offering of intercessory prayer (Iles, 1990, p. 14). Crafting words to reflect this complex fusion of factors, as well as the mutuality between the human and divine, is a demanding calling:

> once we actually try to bring to God the needs of the Church and of the world, we confront head on, almost cruelly, our inability to do all that is so desperately required. Immediately, we are face to face with our human frailty, impotence and helplessness . . . This is the point where the temporary vision of God we are able to sustain regularly collapses and is remade. (pp. 41–2)

The aim of giving attention to the crafting of language in liturgy is to open up the possibility that words can evoke feelings and images: 'presences' which allow worshippers to glimpse a vision of something which is 'out of this world' by leading them beyond the abstract and conceptual. It is an echo of what T. S. Eliot was feeling for in his description of the 'auditory imagination' as

> the feeling for syllable and rhythm, penetrating far below the conscious levels of thought and feeling, invigorating every word; sinking to the most primitive and forgotten, returning to the origin and bringing something back . . . (1933, pp. 118–19)

Silence

Eliot's insight suggests that words have a potency beyond themselves. Words spoken in the liturgy, which '[begin] as an impulse' (Brook, 1968, p. 12; see above, p. 86), have the potential to unlock thoughts and feelings which have otherwise been inhibited, to stimulate the imagination, to face the pressures of life and invite an encounter with the living God.

Language, if used sensitively and resourcefully, should bring worshippers to a moment where (in the words of Vincent van Gogh) they are 'hand to mouth with reality'. A perceptive and empathetic liturgical president will know that such a moment is often possible only when words give way to silence, and space has been created to allow language, once spoken, to be unleashed in the mind and heart of the worshipper.

It is significant that, amid the descriptions of the noise that accompanies the worship of heaven in the book of Revelation, where trumpets sound, massed voices chant and peals of thunder resound, there comes a moment when silence suddenly descends for half an hour (Rev. 8.1ff). Heaven falls silent to listen to the 'prayers of the saints' – the persecuted poor of Asia Minor. This suggests that if our worship on earth is a foretaste of the worship of eternity, all liturgical celebration needs to make space for moments of silent attentiveness; when we not only absorb the words spoken in the liturgy, but allow the cries of our own hearts to be uttered and the voices of the unknown, unseen, unheard millions of our human race to become a conscious presence in our own prayers and longings. By providing worshippers with a 'breathing space' in the overall flow and momentum of the liturgy, a sensitive president will have an innate feel for the way silence enables worshippers to 'hear' what has either been suppressed, ignored or 'talked out' during the rest of the liturgy.

Interestingly, neurological study reveals that, although the left hemisphere of the brain deals with the processing of language, the right hemisphere (the 'silent partner' as Iain McGilchrist describes it) makes sense of its significance. The right hemisphere, which deals with the implicit, enables us to understand what others mean and to express the meaning of words; as well as enabling us to grasp the moral of a story or the punchline of a joke. So in the liturgy, there needs to be a mechanism to enable the significance of what is heard and seen to be extended and enhanced – and this is where creating moments of silence becomes crucial.

Just as some liturgical presidents are possessed of a compulsion to explain (see pp. 73ff), others are simply compelled to talk – and keep talking! Account needs to be taken of the impact of words in creating 'aural fatigue' among worshippers: there comes a point where a congregation cannot take any more. Those of us who preach with any sensitivity will instinctively know when 'saturation point' has been reached and a congregation begins to 'glaze over'. Similarly, those who preside at the liturgy need to cultivate a focused empathy to discern when speech, which has triggered unspoken thoughts and feelings, should end and silence must begin. If a liturgical president is uncomfortable with silence, and the discipline of being still and attentive is alien to a president's own practice of prayer, it is probably going to be a challenge to encourage the practice in those being led in worship. Liturgical presidency calls for a degree of insight and perceptiveness, to know that, very often, the silences worshippers may need are longer than we imagine; that worshippers may be deprived of an essential dimension of their engagement with God when a president imposes limits on silence. In a culture of busyness and addiction to urgency, it is all to easy to allow space for silence with a grudging inevitability before rushing to the next thing. And yet

> it is a good idea to allow God as long as God wants. How long is that? Who knows? But it would be surprising if a God of such abundance, who longs to communicate in love, could be satisfied with brief set times. It is easy to find ourselves treating God less generously than we treat our best friend, our spouse or those we serve in our work. In all those relationships we recognize occasions when whatever is going on has to take as long as it takes. (Ford, 1997, p. 90)

At every celebration of the Eucharist, there will be worshippers who may be overwhelmed by the language and symbols they encounter in the liturgy; or who may bring with them experiences of life which are simply overwhelming. David Ford, drawing on the model of Ezekiel by the River Chebar (Ezek.

3.12–16) has explored how the 'multiple overwhelmings' of life can find a measure of catharsis and resolution in practices which do not rely on words alone (1997, pp. 174ff). Faced with the overwhelming of his exiled people, Ezekiel finds he can say no more; he simply sits among his people for seven days and absorbs the immensity of what has happened. Ford suggests that, in contemporary culture, any number of factors might overwhelm those who come to worship, including economic pressures, sex and a vast range of gender-related issues, addiction, obsessions to do with staying young, fit and beautiful, discrimination and violence and the overwhelming impact of information inundating us from social media and IT on an hourly basis, as well as that ultimate overwhelming, death. Not all experiences are adverse, of course, and there will be those who are overwhelmed by the unfettered joy of having fallen in love, given birth, overcome a life-threatening illness, attained a long-hoped-for achievement in their personal or professional lives. Rarely can words alone provide an outlet for such feelings and emotions.

This is where creating significant moments of silence in the liturgy becomes as vital as choices about language. Silence allows worshippers to use their aural faculties differently: to hear things that a constant flow of words may be eliminating. It can allow the use of the eyes (to give uninterrupted attention to the worshipping space, its symbols and sculptures and to those who worship alongside us). Above all, it can create a more concentrated awareness of the self in relation to God: of how the contours of our immediate experiences of life are echoed in the narrative of scripture, or the shape and language of the liturgy.

It is vital for liturgical presidents to appreciate that silence is as appropriate for celebration as for sorrow. In a culture where worship and entertainment are often confused, the dimension of silence is one way in which the drama of the liturgy can be invested with added significance and marked out as distinctive. Significantly, it is from the experience of directing theatre production that Peter Brook offers a compelling case for silence as part of the overall impact of the liturgical celebration:

We do not know how to celebrate because we do not know what to celebrate. All we know is the end result: we know and we like the feel and sound of celebration through applause, and this where we get stuck. We forget that there are two possible climaxes to a theatre experience. There is the climax of celebration in which our participation explodes in stamping and cheering, shouts of hurrah and the roar of hands, or else, at the other end of the stick, the climax of silence – another form of recognition and appreciation for an experience shared. We have largely forgotten silence. It even embarrasses us; we clap our hands mechanically because we do not know what else to do, and we are unaware that silence is also permitted, that silence is also good. (1968, p. 47)

From speech and silence, we now move to consider how liturgical actions can 'speak' louder than words.

4

Hearts and Hands and Voices: When Words are Never Enough

> The world too deep for speech, the silent world of symbolic action . . . is the answer to an inner need . . . The most deeply moving moments of our lives usually leave us speechless, and in such moments our body carriage may well be able to express what would otherwise be inexpressible. (Laban, 1971, p. 9)

The suburb of Leeds where I spent my early childhood is home to a large Jewish community, with several orthodox synagogues. I have clear memories from that time of a delivery van, bearing the Star of David, arriving at the home of a Jewish school friend who lived just a few doors away. One of his grandparents had died that morning, and I stood outside his house with a growing sense of fascination and curiosity as a large number of small chairs were taken into the house, and the chairs I recognized as coming from the family dining room and kitchen were put in the van and driven off. Sometime later, I plucked up the courage to ask my friend's mother why they had swapped chairs. I was given a striking demonstration of a crucial element in the Jewish ritual of bereavement. As she brought one of these chairs from another part of the house, she sat on it and, although only about eight years old at the time, I seemed to tower above her as she sat barely a few inches from the floor. She went on to explain that, when sad or grieving, we talk about 'feeling down' or 'being brought low'. Jews, she said, do not simply talk or think about how they feel or what they believe: they express it with their bodies and by their actions. As if it to amplify the point, my friend's mother went to fetch her husband's suit jacket, in which there was an untidy tear near the breast pocket. Again, she told me how we talk about feeling 'cut to the heart' when we grieve over the death of a loved one; but Jews demonstrate it in a physical and concrete manner. Finally, she showed me some eggs and bagels and talked about the meal they ate when they returned from the cemetery, where all the food is circular to symbolize the continuity of life after death. Jews *perform* their grief as well as speaking and hearing about it.

Language and Gesture

This childhood discovery of the Jewish *Shiveh* ritual enabled me, in time, to grasp a primal anthropological insight which underlines a vital dimension of human development: that language has not always been necessary for communication. Neurological study has shown that the area of the brain that stimulates the mechanisms required for language also stimulates manual skills; and the skills needed for speech production are the same as those required for hand movements. It can be seen in the early speech development of babies, for example, where naming is invariably accompanied by pointing. Similarly, a young woman who was born without upper limbs experiences 'phantom' limb gestures when she speaks because her speaking activates the area of the brain that stimulates the limbs. So close is the similarity that at least one theory has suggested that 'referential language may have evolved, not from sounds at all, but actually direct from hand movements' (McGilchrist, 2009, p. 111).

Similarly, studies of primitive sub-Saharan African cultures have revealed how information can be conveyed over long distances by rhythm (usually drum-beats). The actual rhythmic patterns used in a message may be known only to one tribe, and not to others. This presents an obvious and immediate challenge. If you cannot understand the rhythmic 'code', how do you decipher and interpret drum-beats heard over long distances? The key to interpreting the meaning of the rhythm lies in the ability to 'picture' the body movements – and especially the manual actions – of the drummer. Only when the drummer's physical movements are imagined and visualized is the meaning of the message fully grasped.

Many Western artists before the Reformation communicate the underlying character of their work and the many subtleties of meaning through their portrayal of body language. Titian's *Noli Me Tangere*[1] is one of the classic depictions of the encounter between the risen Christ and Mary Magdalene on Easter morning; and the artist perfectly captures the tension of this encounter, present in the written Gospel account, by the way he has chosen to portray Christ's body language. It is an intensely tender depiction of the Johannine account of the Easter morning encounter and vividly coveys both deep desire and nervous withdrawal. The assurance to Mary that Christ has been raised from the dead, coupled to his stern admonition that she cannot touch him because death has changed the nature of his physical presence, is signified by the curve of his body. Christ appears as if he is both drawing back from Mary's outstretched arm whilst also leaning over and towards her in a reciprocal gesture of desire. Here is invitation and withdrawal, as if one world is ending and another is coming into being. This body tells its own story, and its language invites enquiry and discovery.

If the body and the movement of the body provides the perspective from which much basic human experience is expressed and communicated, it will be apparent that the relationship between speech, language and gesture is a vital one for those who preside at the liturgy. When account is taken of the natural human inclination towards worship (whether in church, a sports stadium, or a relationship of love), it becomes evident that the dramatic, musical and even dance-like qualities of liturgical celebration demand significant non-verbal expression. Many stage directors have identified the degree to which an audience will subconsciously distil the meaning of a performance through the body movements of a performer and, even when those

---

1 www.nationalgallery.org.uk/paintings/titian-noli-me-tangere.

movements are unconventional, they often have the power to impress or inspire. This may be one of the reasons why Rowan Atkinson's iconic portrayal of the television character 'Mr Bean' has been so successfully exported around the world: precisely because the characterization relies so heavily on body language which makes the meaning accessible to different cultures.

This is an insight which Eucharistic presidents can profitably embrace when leading an act of worship which has a fundamental theological focus on the body, particularly in the words spoken and the gestures enacted over the bread and cup: this my *body* . . . The presence of Christ is encountered in the Eucharist through a striking physicality, when words and bodily gestures combine to take on a consecratory quality. A similar dimension can be discerned in weddings, for example, where the marriage is enacted, not just by saying legally or sacramentally recognized words, but by physical actions such as joining hands and the giving and receiving of rings. Sacramental reality is enacted by words *and* actions.

Gesture as Authentic Expression

The question of how speech and bodily action are expressed in the liturgy is most obviously located in the confidence (as well as being hampered by the uncertainty) with which gestures accompany different liturgical texts. This is not a book which seeks to espouse a particular partisan approach to liturgical gestures, to champion a supposedly 'correct' practice, or impose a standardized mode of performing manual or other bodily actions.[2] Nonetheless, it is vital that, if gestures are to correspond to the texts they seek to amplify, and if they are to convey the drama as well as the theology of the rite with any degree of

---

2 Those concerned with replicating the manual actions and other gestures prescribed in the Roman Missal, for example, should consult Adrian Fortescue, 2009. An 'Anglican Translation' specific to *Common Worship* may be found in Benjamin Gordon-Taylor and Simon Jones, 2005.

authenticity, it is helpful if presidents have a strong sense of how these gestures have evolved over time and in relation to the historical development of the liturgy. In other words, those who preside at the Eucharist should possess a reasonably confident grasp of the historical and theological significance of the basic choreography of the rite, simply because the celebration of the Eucharist is never a purely local or contemporary undertaking: it is an expression of the Church's catholicity. Any sense of 'this is how *I* do it' or 'this is what works for *me*' has the potential to reduce and limit the Church's defining act of worship to an individual or congregational activity. It needs to be remembered that those who preside do so to express not merely a personal perspective, but the corporate, historic practice of the Church.

Of equal importance is the question of how an understanding of the physical gestures and signs used in the liturgy are recognized and interpreted by the Church today. This will enable presidents to make intelligent and informed decisions about appropriate choices and the level of gesture to be employed in the liturgy. This is especially germane when multifarious practices can be observed in different arenas, most often by those whose criteria for liturgical gesture are based either on a misreading of good practice, a paucity in understanding the history and use of liturgical gesture, or merely on what works for the individual rather than a concern to express the corporate tradition of the Church. If each celebration of the Eucharist is recognized as 'an obscure, mysterious, organic process whereby you give birth to a performance which is highly delicate, extremely vulnerable and has to be produced afresh every time', the president will have grasped something of how they both embody the tradition and employ that embodiment as a crucial part of expressing the tradition of the Church and the proclamation of the Gospel that is entrusted to them.

About ten years ago, anyone travelling on the commuter rail routes radiating out of Dublin would have seen a notice on the window of each carriage with the words 'seats are not for feet' – accompanied by the symbol of a lighted cigarette, enclosed in a circle, with a diagonal line across it!

This is a neat parable of what happens, liturgically, when symbols and gestures are employed on a seemingly random basis, when there is little connection between what is said and what is seen and there is a failure to 'read' accurately the cultural or social context in which those words and symbols are employed. Where words and gestures seem ill-at-ease in the liturgy, it often arises from an absence of historical, theological, spatial or aesthetic awareness. A president's liturgical bearing will be helped significantly if it is recognized that the use of symbolic body language is not primarily about reproducing or imitating the body language of everyday life (walking down the street, drinking coffee, or relaxing in front of the television, etc.); it requires an awareness that what is being enacted in the liturgy may, at first sight, seem strange or inexplicable and will attract further scrutiny and reflection. The body language of liturgical action may use the same physical actions and attributes of everyday movement; but because it happens in particular sequences and rhythms, it expresses beliefs, feelings and insights which are far from the everyday. In this way, body language has the capacity to be more effective, for the long term, than functional or prosaic verbal explanations.

Two Basic Movements

The choreographer, Rudolph Laban, has identified two basic body movements which provide the basis for most dance forms. The first starts from the centre of the body and moves outwards into space. The second begins far away from the body and moves inwards towards its centre. The first of these basic movements is described as 'scattering' and the second as 'gathering'. These descriptions are deeply suggestive for the celebration of the Eucharist, where the shape and movement of the Eucharist in the West is characterized by a linear movement from gathering to scattering (or dismissal). As Laban goes on to suggest, these basic movements can then assume a more complex character as the two basic forms are combined in different

sequences and movements. This, too, is analogous to the different moments of significance in the flow and momentum of the
Eucharistic celebration (see Laban, 1971, pp. 83ff).

Before moving on to explore some specific examples of
body language, it might be helpful to highlight a more general,
but widespread, experience of the physical nature of liturgical presidency: fatigue. Presiding at the Eucharist is physically demanding. Those who speak of feeling 'washed out'
after presiding, not just at a principal Sunday celebration, but
also at weekday services which are smaller in scale, will have
experienced something of the cost and demands of exercising such a ministry. It is one of the most tangible ways in
which Eucharistic presidency is an expression of being *in loco
Christi* – of signifying that the president stands in the place
of Christ, 'whose arms of love / aching, spent, the world sustain'.[3] The combination of vocal projection, breath control,
adopting postures which require sustained effort, standing
unsupported for extended periods, as well as the mental concentration required (even when sitting or apparently 'doing
nothing') combine to make Eucharistic presidency an exact-
ing undertaking. Such insights will come as little surprise to
those who 'perform' in the public arena, whether as actors,
musicians, politicians or teachers. Sounds and gestures are
dependent upon precise physical movements.

In his consideration of the physical character of mime, for
example, Rudolph Laban strikingly suggests that it is analogous to the interdependence of prayer and work (which is an
ideal memorably embodied in *The Rule of St Benedict*) and
that all artistic endeavour has its roots in worship:

> The roots of mime are work and prayer . . . Work is akin
> to prayer when it is done not solely to maintain life but for
> a higher purpose. An artistic performance on stage setting
> forth an ideal can thus be very near to prayer. Prayer can be
> closely allied with work. The building up of ideals, as is often

---

3 'Hymn to the Creator', in Vanstone, 1977, p. 112.

done by fervent prayer, may be just as hard work or even harder work, than manual labour. It may entail the full use of all our energy. The conflicts arising in work and prayer are represented in mine, drama and dance. In ancient times, dramatic poetry, and dance linked with music, developed from worship; and in modern times this is still the true order of development. (1971, p. 90)

Shared Basics

Broadly, there are four levels of manual gesture which the Western Church has, historically, employed in the celebration of the Eucharist. They should be regarded as both organic and instinctive; and suggest their meaning best when performed in an unforced and spontaneous manner which betrays a president's sense of being 'at home' in the liturgical arena.

Making Welcome

Grace, mercy and peace from God our Father
and the Lord Jesus Christ be with you
All   **and also with you.**

The peace of the Lord be always with you.
All   **and also with you.**

The Lord be with you.
All   **And also with you.**

The gesture of greeting and invitation is a presidential –
presbyteral or episcopal (as opposed to a diaconal or auxiliary) – gesture. It happens most obviously at the beginning
of worship when the formal liturgical greeting is given, when
the greeting is given at the exchange of the Peace and at the
beginning of the Eucharistic Prayer. The impression created
in Jan Struther's hymn 'Lord of all hopefulness' evokes the
character of this gesture: 'your hands swift to welcome, your
arms to embrace'. A generous extending of the arms, conveying a readiness to give or receive, is called for; along with a
suggestion that worshippers are being drawn out of themselves into a much wider dimension of space, time and relat-
edness. Elbows should be comfortably away from the side of
the body, and the palms of the hands should be orientated
towards the congregation. This is very different, for example,
from the 'Angel of the North' posture where arms and fingers
are rigidly extended sideways from the body (like children
impersonating an aeroplane) or the more minimal extending
of the arms to no more than the width of the torso, with
elbows firmly against the side of the body and the palms of
the hands facing each other.

   In practice, this gesture tends to suffer from over-use (and is
often confused with the second gesture described below). Such
over-use dilutes and diminishes the power of the meaning it
seeks to suggest. Some liturgical presidents convey the impression that it is a gesture to use *ad libitum* whenever they are

speaking. It is a gesture that has been observed, unhelpfully, when leading congregational prayers (e.g. the Prayers of Penitence), when reading the Gospel and even when reciting the Creed.

Prayer

Lift up your hearts.
All   **We lift them to the Lord.**

Let us give thanks to the Lord our God.
All   **It is right to give thanks and praise.**

Lord, you are holy indeed, the source of all holiness . . .

And so, Father, calling to mind his death on the cross, his perfect sacrifice made once for the sins of the whole world; rejoicing in his mighty resurrection and glorious ascension, and looking for his coming in glory, we celebrate this memorial of our redemption.

As we offer you this our sacrifice of praise and thanksgiving, we bring before you this bread and this cup and we thank you for counting us worthy to stand in your presence and serve you. (*CW*, Eucharistic Prayer B)

Most merciful God,
who by the death and resurrection of your Son Jesus Christ
delivered and saved the world:
grant that by faith in him who suffered on the cross
we may triumph in the power of his victory;
through Jesus Christ your Son our Lord,
who is alive and reigns with you,
in the unity of the Holy Spirit,
one God, now and for ever.

(*CW*, Collect for Fifth Sunday of Lent)

A second gesture, called *orans* (from the Latin 'to pray'), is similar to, but distinct from, the greeting and welcome gesture. It is used when speaking Presidential Prayers (Collect, Eucharistic Prayer, Presidential Post-Communion Prayer). It is a gesture that calls for an extending of the arms, with elbows a little closer to the body and with the palms of the hands turned upwards. The gesture models the ancient Jewish practice of prayer (and so is also traditionally used when reciting the Lord's Prayer at the Eucharist to echo the probable practice of Jesus and his contemporaries – even though this prayer has become a congregational text in modern rites). It echoes the words of Psalm 141: 'Let my prayer rise before you as incense, and the lifting up of my hands as an evening sacrifice.' This is a weighty gesture, which signifies the president making prayer on behalf of the congregation, and its frequently observed use during congregational texts (Collect for Purity, congregational Post-Communion Prayer, etc.) significantly weakens its impact.

Invoking

Grant that by the power of your Holy Spirit, and according to your holy will, these gifts of bread and wine may be to us the body and blood of our Lord Jesus Christ . . .

Send the Holy Spirit on your people and gather into one in your kingdom all who share this one bread and one cup, so that we, in the company of all the saints, may praise and glorify you for ever, through Jesus Christ our Lord . . . (CW, Eucharistic Prayer B)

Now sanctify this water that, by the power of your Holy Spirit,
they may be cleansed from sin and born again . . .
          (CW, Baptism rite at the Blessing of the Water)

A third gesture is one of invoking the Holy Spirit (over the gifts during the Eucharistic Prayer, during the Prayer over the

Water at baptism, when praying over candidates at Confirmation, blessing of the rings at Marriage, etc.).

Traditionally called *epiklesis* (from the Greek to 'call down'), the arms are extended in front of the president, with elbows close to the body and palms facing down over the gifts (or the element which is the focus of the prayer). The gesture may have developed from some oriental liturgies, where a fan is used during the prayer to call down the Spirit over the bread and wine at the Eucharist, and this most obviously seeks to draw out the imagery of the wind of the Spirit and the tongues of fire descending on the apostles, as described in Acts 2. It also evokes the wings of the cherubim and seraphim described in the Temple vision of Isaiah 6, notably highlighted in some Easter liturgies, such as the Syrian Liturgy of St James:

Let all mortal flesh keep silent,
and with fear and trembling stand.
Ponder nothing earthly-minded,
for the King of kings and Lord of lords
advances to be slain and given as food to the faithful.
Before him go the choirs of angels,
with every rule and authority,
the many-eyed Cherubim and the six-winged Seraphim,
veiling their sight and crying out the hymn: Alleluia, Alleluia, Alleluia.

It is a gesture whose significance is heightened by very sparing use.

Some presidents tend to use it twice when reciting Eucharistic Prayers containing a 'double *epiklesis*' (a prayer calling down the Spirit on the people as well as the gifts), such as CW, Eucharist Prayer B. In this second use, the palms of the hands face towards the congregation rather than the gifts on the altar, with the hands spaced further apart and the elbows a little further away from the sides of the body.

Together

A fourth gesture is the one of joined hands (either clasped, or with fingers extended, palms pressed together and thumbs crossed, with elbows close to the side of the body and the hands held at abdominal level). This gesture conveys an attitude of prayer. It is a gesture rarely used in everyday life in the Northern hemisphere (though it is common in Indian cultures, for example) and indicates that the liturgical environment is a 'set apart' place. Hands should be joined whenever walking or moving from place to place (e.g. in processions or from the Presidential Chair to the lectern). During worship, a president's arms should *never* be allowed to swing by their sides. Hands should be joined while standing when someone else is speaking a text or performing a liturgical action. It is a gesture to be employed when leading texts spoken by the whole congregation, when reading the scriptures (including the Gospel), when speaking words of invitation to confession, and so on.

Suggesting what traditional manual actions the president might employ to accompany particular texts at various points in the liturgy is merely a basic starting point. These gestures need to be part of a pattern of pace and flow. If comprehensible speech requires much more than isolated words or phrases, but

also structured, coherent and progressive sentences, it f
that physical movements and gestures require logical sec
which also communicate non-verbal meaning and significance.
Gestures also need to be enacted with confidence and conviction, as if they are inherent to the character of the person who
embodies and performs them.

Throughout the drama of the Eucharist, the president is
called to hold the celebration together visibly and symbolically,
even when apparently 'doing nothing'. The attitude needs to be
one of attentive engagement with everything that is taking place
and a clear modelling of that attentiveness to all those who
participate in the liturgy. The impression given needs to evoke
Martin Buber's observation that, 'if you look at life intensely
and hallow it, you cannot but fail to meet God' (2004, p. 79).

From the Beginning

From the outset of the liturgical action, the president's body
language is vital in signalling the magnitude of what is about
to unfold in the liturgy. This will be helped by an unself-
conscious focus away from him/herself, summoning the attention of worshippers away from themselves and by leading their
attention towards the arena which is to become the focus of
worship. The manner in which a president walks towards the
arena of worship, whether as part of a long procession with
other ministers, or over a short distance alone, should evoke
a sense of gravity. An initial bow to the altar or the cross, for
example, should be a clear gesture which expresses the whole
congregation's adoration; and should, significantly, employ the
whole body as an expression of the conviction, expressed in Isaac
Watts' hymn, that the Christian sacrifice of praise 'demands
my soul, my life, my all'.

A perfunctory 'nod' will never adequately express this. To
bow the body in worship towards a physical object is not, as
some might suggest, an act of idolatry. It is to acknowledge
that the altar or the cross can be a commonly acknowledged

focus for an encounter with the living Christ to whom 'all knees shall bow' (Phil. 2.10). It is also to acknowledge where true authority in this world is located for Christian worshippers and to express a sense of overwhelming and fascination at the reality of God. Above all, it is to indicate – especially at the outset of worship – who we most truly are in relation to God (especially in our need of healing and forgiveness which makes us entirely dependent upon the infinite mercy of God).

What may seem like initial, subsidiary gestures by the president are vital in setting the tone of worship, which is why deliberately measured and paced actions must be clearly observable and never visually cluttered, obscured by furnishings or eclipsed by a phalanx of assisting ministers. Similarly, the gestures that accompany the opening words of the liturgy (sign of the cross, greeting, confessing, absolving, praying) need to be deliberate and confident, without any suggestion that they are an afterthought, a source of confusion or a cause for embarrassment.

Above all, a president's demeanour at the outset of the liturgy needs to convey a sense of composure and confident stillness: a readiness to inaugurate the Church's sacrifice of praise with a measure of humanity which also signifies the worshipping community's proximity to the threshold of heaven. This becomes significant when many presidents have been observed adopting two contrasting postures at the start of the liturgy. When speaking and expressing the 'scripted' text of the liturgy (e.g. the greeting or pronouncing the absolution) they can exemplify a sturdy confidence in their task. But when speaking 'off script' (e.g. introducing the Prayers of Penitence in their own words) they adopt a completely different posture which conveys a lack of confidence or lack of preparation, by leaning forward or moving their weight from one side of their body to the other. It is an indication that any 'improvised' text needs to be spoken or enacted with the same degree of confidence as the rest of the liturgy (see p. 82).

Sitting Target

To preside at the liturgy is, by definition, to 'sit before' those who are being led in worship. Therefore, attention needs to be focused as much on what impression is conveyed when the president is sitting down (to listen to the scriptures being read, when someone else preaching, or in leading a significant moment of silence after communion) as it is on speech and gesture. The Presidential Chair, along with the lectern/pulpit and the altar, is a principal component of liturgical furniture in every church. Placing the Presidential Chair in a visible, even central, location will help to emphasize that there is a clear connection between presidency and visibility (see p. 17). Although this will depend on the architecture of the building (see Chapter 5), the careful placing of the presidential seat will signify that it is the president's task to enable the celebration to take place, to enable others to exercise an appropriate ministry within the liturgy and to model for all worshippers a pattern of full and active participation in the entire liturgical action. This is an essential dynamic of liturgical leadership: not that the president does *everything*; but, instead, enables the worship of the whole people of God to take place. This should be a matter of restrained self-confidence in the role, rather than any desire to dominate. To be seated in an out-of-the-way location, or 'to the side' may undermine this sense of presidential visibility; it could also be interpreted as a sign of either insecurity in the role the president is called to embody, a misplaced *faux* humility or even a superficial, one-dimensional expression of 'collaboration'.

When seated, the president should adopt an attentive, upright posture and should not be causing a distraction to other worshippers by 'catching-up' due to earlier lack of preparation (flicking-through the pages of a book, fiddling with glasses, adjusting a microphone, talking to other ministers or even looking around the building in a distracted manner). The president's eyes should be resolutely focused on the liturgical action taking place – especially when it is being performed by someone else. When a president sits with legs crossed, arms folded or even slumped in the Presidential Chair, it simply conveys the impression of boredom; or worse, an attitude of casualness towards the liturgical action which not only diminishes the significance of the worship of the people of God, but trivializes the liturgical ministry of others. It is vital that a president's body language should challenge any notion that the liturgy is a medium of entertainment; or that, unless a liturgical action is being performed by the president, it is somehow superficial. This applies particularly to facial expressions, especially in reaction to what is being said and sung, or actions performed by others. Raised eyebrows, winces and sharp intakes of breath – especially in reaction to the actions or mistakes of others – are often more visible (and audible) than we imagine!

Footwork

What is true of hands and eyes applies correspondingly to feet. The Psalmist's recognition that God has set our feet in a large space (Psalm 31.8) suggests that places of worship are not only distinctive as a set-apart environment for divine encounter, but are also large enough to facilitate transience and movement. In other words, the liturgical arena is not only a destination in its own right, but a staging-post on a longer route to somewhere, ultimately, not of this world. What happens in worship points to another, eternal destination. How a president chooses to 'walk about Zion' (Psalm 48.12) should evoke a sense of both sanctuary and of pilgrimage: a belief that we are not only being called *into* a holy place; but also being called to *move beyond* it – both for mission and service in this world and to participate in the heavenly banquet in the next.

The general *pace* at which the president walks in worship should be strikingly different from the pace adopted in other areas of life. Worship is an activity like no other, and the pace adopted should be quite unlike either a frantic rush to catch a train or idle loitering at a bus stop. Equally, this difference should not become an excuse to cultivate a clerical 'glide' or a liturgical 'swagger'. Instead, a sense that the courts of the Lord are being trodden and that our feet are being placed in the footprints of those who have walked this way before us, should result in a purposeful sense of movement from where you are to where you are heading. If each movement is accompanied by hands clasped at the level of the abdomen, with eyes firmly fixed on the intended destination, the right impression will be created.

The tendency, when walking in worship (e.g. in a procession through the congregation), to catch someone's eye, accompanied by smiles, smirks, winks and other facial gestures, can easily undermine the gravity of the role the president embodies. It not only encourages frivolity (which is often born of embarrassment and insecurity) but inevitably signals a superficiality which is out of kilter with the tenor the president seeks to establish for the whole worshipping community. Alongside these considerations, of course, is the hugely important dimension of how a president's body language conveys an authentic sense of their own humanity (see p. 32), but this will not be appropriately achieved by a frequent evocation of flippancy.

Obviously, the size of the building also has a considerable bearing on the pace at which the president and other ministers walk. A long procession through a large cathedral with a congregation of many hundreds will require a degree of momentum and a more animated tempo; whereas a smaller space, with a smaller number of liturgical participants moving through it, will require something more measured and deliberate. This is where a president needs to develop a keen sense of spatial awareness and to feel 'at home' in a particular building, so that their physical movements are allowed to be in harmony with (and in proportion to) their architectural surroundings.

Similarly, the *placing of feet* when standing is also significant. Just as it will feel out of place – and probably physically unsustainable – to adopt too rigid a posture (as if standing to attention at a military parade), so it will be similarly inappropriate to rock or sway from side to side. By placing the feet slightly apart, the need to keep distributing body weight from one foot to the other is avoided, and a suitably 'relaxed formal' posture can be achieved. This also helps considerably with breath control when speaking or singing texts. Adopting a similar posture when keeping silence (after 'Let us pray' before the Collect, for example) helps considerably in creating an impression of focused stillness.

It is significant, for example, that any good actor, instrumentalist or singer will devote as much attention to the *physical* preparation for a performance as they do to the specifically musical or vocal technique, timbre, rhythm, pitch, intonation or volume and dynamics. Most people who belong to good choirs, for example, should spend up to 20 per cent of their total rehearsal time beginning with exercises to help relax the body, improve breath control, adopt an appropriate posture and generally prepare their bodies to be an 'instrument' through which the intentions of the composer are brought to life.[4] The implication for a liturgical president is that audibility needs to be accompanied by a deliberately directed and developed physicality.

Blessing

The final gesture of the Eucharistic action expresses – and opens up – many meanings. In the ancient Semitic cultures of the East, from which Christianity emerged, the patriarch of the household, the ruler of a tribe or the monarch would bless those in his care or under his protection as a pledge of future security. It was – and is – a sign of well-being, of right relationship to God and the continuity of the blessings of life. At the conclusion of the Eucharist, the sustaining and

---

4 Examples of 'warm-up' exercises for singers may be found in Hill, 2007.

transforming quality of the sacrament is 'written in the air' as the visible sign by which worshippers are sent out of worship to live their baptismal commission. The president pronounces the blessing with a clear underlying sense of the connection between the dismissal of the worshippers and the signing of the cross in baptism, with its challenge to 'remain faithful to Christ to the end of your life' which is the foundation of their participation in the *Missio Dei*. The deliberate signing of the departing worshippers with the cross in blessing is also a symbol that enables them, in the words of W. H. Vanstone's hymn, to 'tell of what God's love must be' as the cross, a sign of healing, forgiveness, strength and inexhaustible love, is given to them to authorize and sustain them in the fulfilment of their vocation.

Crossing Predispositions

Until relatively recently, one of the visible signs that identify someone as being Catholic (or Orthodox), or not, was the making of the sign of the cross – whether in blessing or by an individual on their body as a gesture of devotion. Against the landscape of post-Reformation Europe in particular, the sign of humanity's reconciliation with God has been a divisive gesture (typified, perhaps, by the way a Catholic entering a pub in a Protestant area of Belfast or Glasgow would be identified by others making a *faux* sign of the cross when their back was turned). In the final decades of the twentieth century, this symbolic partition has become less pronounced in the churches. The sign of the cross has become more widespread in the Church of England, under the influence of the Catholic Revival; and its use has been advocated by different expressions of 'Protestant' Christianity, for example the Swiss Reformed Pastor, Brother Roger of Taizé and the English Methodist Gordon Wakefield (1983, p. 347).

Nonetheless, among those presiding at the liturgy who have not been formed within a broadly catholic spirituality (or received their training and formation at an institution with a catholic identity), there exists a measure of ambivalence, confusion or uncertainty about the appropriateness of this gesture. However, it is one of the primary signs of Christian identity – and not just because it is used by the majority of the world's Christians. It is a sign that takes us back to our origins – personally and historically – as we are marked with the cross before baptism when, in the waters, we die and rise with Christ. As with all signs and gestures, it conveys many different levels of meaning, which are as much cultural as they are theological. Frequently, the sign of the cross is made with water, as Christians enter churches, as a reminder of their own baptism: 'in the name of the Father, and of the Son, and of the Holy Spirit'. This baptismal origin means that its use in other contexts is often a means of expressing a Christian identity in a concrete and physical way. Like the other physical gestures used when presiding at the Eucharist, making the sign of the cross may, at first, seem (and feel) awkward and unfamiliar; but maybe it should evoke a measure of discomfort – not least because the cross suggests not only pain, but also a measure of being counter-cultural towards the values of society which are at odds with a Christian vision of justice and peace.

Many Anglican liturgies now begin with an evocation of the Trinity which calls for the making of the sign of the cross. In the truest sense, this is an archaic sign and recalls the worshipping community to its distinctive Christian character and its origins in baptism – because it is only by being baptized that we are enabled to receive the sacramental elements of the Eucharist. Just as we begin our Christian life with the sign of the cross, so we begin our worship. By making the sign of the cross on significant points of the body, a Christian is bearing witness to the truth that (in Brother Roger's words) salvation touches every part of us. And, as baptism is not an end but a beginning whose effects sustains us throughout our Christian pilgrimage, so the making of the sign of the cross can nourish the sense that the whole human being is caught up in the redemptive and life-giving power of the cross – which is a primary impetus for the celebration of the Eucharist.

Voicing Creation's Praise and Humanity's Lament

The imaginative use of the voice, like other parts of the body, is vital to the totality of presiding at the liturgy. It simply is not sufficient to be able to project the voice and maintain a basic level of breath control, in order to achieve a uniform register, volume and tone. Not every text, gesture and moment of the liturgy is similarly uniform, and the voice is as important in tracing the contours of the liturgical action as music, spaces, symbols and gestures. The human voice, like a musical instrument, is capable of a phenomenally wide-ranging level of expression; and the voice of the president will need to be 'coloured' in different ways and at different points in the overall flow of the liturgy.

The voice is, essentially, a movement or gesture that has become audible, and it is used in liturgy to express emotion and significance and to echo the contours of the evolving liturgical drama. And, while care needs to be taken to do this by degrees if anything of the melodramatic is to be avoided, there also needs to be a keen awareness of the extent to which the use of the voice expresses thought and aspiration, conveys deeper levels of meaning, or can heighten tension and indicate resolution. In short, the president's voice needs to convey something of their understanding of the shape, content, symbols and gestures of the liturgy at which they preside. This is especially germane when account is taken of the observation that speech cannot exist in isolation from bodily tension and movement and that words can be as easily filled with music and movement as a song or an opera. As the veteran English soprano Janet Baker has suggested, the human voice (whether in speech or song) is a means to expressing an inner, previously unspoken urge.

At a fundamental level, sensitive and imaginative presidents will be able to inhabit a basic three-dimensional 'model' of the liturgy, which enables them to recognize the significant moments of the rite at which they preside: the peaks and troughs; the points of praise and penitence; the need for silence or exuberance. This, in turn, will provide a rudimentary 'mental score' which can indicate or suggest the register, pitch, volume and sonority at which particular texts are spoken – or sung. And if this can happen with an underlying appreciation that, like a musical score, the overall liturgical drama builds towards a point of climax and then resolves, this will considerably inform the president's choice of vocal colouring at different moments in the Eucharistic action.

Nonetheless, presiding at the Eucharist is never a 'solo performance' (either for the president or for others who exercise an authorized ministry at different points of the liturgy). As well as obvious moments of vocal dialogue, there is throughout a dynamic interdependence of president and congregation where, even when not speaking or singing, people are nonetheless expressing themselves. How a president colours their voice with an appropriate degree of empathy, so as to evoke from a congregation a response which articulates their spoken or unspoken 'urges', is a considerable and valuable skill which contributes to enabling full and active liturgical participation. For example, how might the president's voice be coloured when pronouncing the absolution in order to give proper to emphasis to the assurance of what is already a reality (i.e. the unbounded forgiveness of God) and the assurance that those who are liberated from their fears and failures are already participating in the promise of eternal life?

What is expressed through speech can, of course, be given heightened significance through song, and this is something that Christians seem to have recognized from an early stage in their worshipping life together. Not only are the New Testament epistles peppered with allusions to singing and even contain texts which we might describe as 'hymns', but some of the earliest Christian liturgies, which developed in the oriental cultures of the East, were invariably sung and chanted in their entirety. This practice is echoed in much Islamic and Jewish worship which, similarly, emerged from these cultures, and in the worship of Western monastic communities. Augustine of Hippo's frequently cited aphorism that '[those] who sing pray

twice' indicates the capacity of music (and the musical potential of the human voice) to provide heightened significance to
the celebration of the Christian liturgy.

Alongside the choice of texts, presidents should be bold
about considering how singing can give emphasis to a particular
moment in the liturgy or a seasonal 'tint'. Those worshipping
communities which presuppose that prayer is an exclusively
spoken activity might be occasionally refreshed by the very
strangeness of the juxtaposition of song and silence when the
collect is intoned rather than said, for example. Similarly, to
sing the traditional plainsong dialogue and preface at the start
of the Eucharistic Prayer – especially when it leads seamlessly
from the preceding offertory hymn – can be a persuasive and
evocative way of signalling the degree to which worshippers are
being drawn into the mystery at the heart of the Church. It will
also provide the congregation – as well as the president – with a
musical vocabulary which may aid (as Gabe Huck puts it) 'the
way prayer gets into the voice' (1984, p. 22). In that sense, a
president may discover that, when singing instead of speaking
texts, they are unexpectedly released to discover that there are
unexpected dimension to the way prayer is articulated, which
shocks and surprises the predictable routines and patterns.

The use of the voice – whether in spoken or sung texts – can
be one of the subliminal ways in which a president can ani-
mate a sense of collective identity and unity in a congregation,
without resorting to the imposition of confected or engineered
ideals of what this might be, simply by evoking a sense of collective responsiveness, attentiveness to others and heighten-
ing a congregation's sensitivity to changes in tone, pitch and
rhythm.

And Also With You

While liturgical celebration stands a reasonable chance of
becoming what it is meant to be when the president's manner
of voice and bodily posture is appropriate, in most churches,

the president is joined by others who are also called to exercise a liturgical ministry at the main Sunday celebration (and, in some situations, on weekdays as well). This highlights the extent to which the quality of worship depends on *everyone* who exercises a liturgical ministry having a keen sense of their responsibility to adopt appropriate body language, employ gestures appropriate to their ministry and to comport themselves in a manner that facilitates (not undermines) the overall quality of worship. What has been said about the need for the president to adopt a posture of focused attentiveness equally holds true for other liturgical ministers – lay and ordained – and any healthy worshipping community will have some mechanism for ensuring that this is so.

The emphasis on collaborative approaches to ministry training over several decades, which has been positively employed in patterns of mission and ministry in local churches, is often most visibly expressed in the principal act of worship on Sundays. At its best, this can express what the Church is called to be, as outlined in 1 Corinthians 12. It has imbued the liturgy with a proper representative character and has enabled many people to employ their gifts in the nurture and growth of the whole body of Christ. It has also enabled good presidency to be modelled in relation to other authorized and locally discerned ministries. Above all, it has diluted the perception that liturgical leadership is an exclusively clerical activity.

Discernment

However, it is also possible to detect a good deal of misjudged and inappropriate patterning when it comes to exercising supportive or auxiliary liturgical ministries. Where this has been frequently observed, it often seems to spring from a fundamental fear of not conforming to the 'orthodoxy of the moment' than from any wholesale confidence in the distinctive vocation being expressed by a particular ministry – whether by the president or another minister. This points to the need for careful discernment, taking time to recognize the appropriate gifts and disposition of those who might be invited to exercise a liturgical ministry, employing a measure of imaginative insight as to how a person might react and respond to the responsibility that comes with exercising a representative role, especially where that might involve occupying a visible space in the church building, wearing distinctive clothing, or being given words to speak or actions to perform. Those who gather to worship need to have a measure of confidence that those who are exercising ministry are appropriate people to do so and that the experience of worship will be enriched for the common good.

Appropriate discernment will go a long way towards obviating the possibility that someone will exercise a liturgical ministry because they harbour (often unacknowledged and unchallenged) needs to do so. It will also guard against a president (or local church) providing that person with an outlet that fulfils a need within the liturgical minister, but which can easily diminish the overall quality of worship for the community as a whole. Worship, like any public arena, can become a pretext for the outworking of an individual's pathology – however benign.

Recently, I worshipped at a celebration of the Eucharist in an Anglican cathedral in a capital city outside the UK. The setting was the Lady Chapel at the East end of the cathedral, where the small congregation (in single figures) was seated in niches along the South and North walls of the chapel. The whole area was little more than 5 sqm. When the president arrived to begin the liturgy, he was dressed appropriately for the small setting in alb and stole. He was accompanied by a lay minister (who had been the duty chaplain in the cathedral that morning) dressed in a short-fitting cassock, surplice and blue preaching scarf (which is more appropriately worn for a choir office, e.g. Morning or Evening Prayer, rather than the Eucharist). The president's tone of voice, pace of speech and employment of gestures was appropriate for the space and number of worshippers. The lay minister seemed to think it was his task to set the volume and pace of the congregational responses, which were excessive for the space. When it came to the reading of scripture, the lay minister moved self-consciously to the lectern, took the book off the lectern and moved to one side to read from it, in what seemed like a clear gesture of making himself more visible. When the Peace was exchanged, the lay minister seemed anxious to shake hands and make his presence felt with the small body of worshippers in advance of the president.

This, undoubtedly, sincerely exercised ministry is nonetheless a reasonable caricature of what can happen in countless parish churches, Sunday by Sunday. It points back to a question raised at the beginning of this book (see p. 17) about the degree to which liturgical presidency is a *visible* ministry. Focusing on an assisting minister's comportment and its capacity either to enhance or interrupt the tone and pace being set by the president, and whether their use of voice and body helps to create an appropriate worshipping environment for everyone else, is a necessary component in assessing the overall quality of the liturgy being offered. In any typical celebration of the Eucharist on a Sunday in many parish churches, a president is likely to be ministering in company with other ordained colleagues, authorized lay ministers, servers, a choir or music group and – vitally – a congregation of worshippers. To what extent these auxiliary ministries support the role of president is worthy of some consideration.

Stewards of the Mysteries

The principal 'supporting' role in the Eucharist is expressed through the ministry of the deacon. While it is beyond the scope of this book to offer a detailed exploration of the liturgical ministry of the deacon, it is hoped that some basic hints will contribute to an understanding of how it might relate to the presidential role.

The ministry of the deacon seems to have been a feature of Christian worship and mission since the New Testament era and, historically, it is a ministry that has an established place in the liturgies of the Eastern and Western churches, denoted by distinctive dress, role and gestures. The etymological roots of the title of deacon are embedded in the model of slavery which was a feature of the Roman Empire and other ancient societies. In these cultures slavery, though fundamentally abhorrent to a Christian vision of society, was a necessary element in enabling 'democracy' to function in the Graeco-Roman world, for example, by releasing citizens from the demands of work, to allow them to participate in activities such as government, sport and education. In a similar way, those who exercise a diaconal ministry in the Eucharist do so to enable the president to preside with an appropriate measure of freedom from the burdens of liturgical housekeeping and administration.

Consequently, the liturgical ministry of deacons is one of stewardship, of preparation, emptying and conveying: preparing the congregation for particular moments and actions in the liturgy; preparing the bread and wine before the Eucharistic Prayer; emptying and clearing the vessels after the celebration; dismissing the congregation and conveying the Eucharistic elements to the sick and housebound after the worship is complete. It is also a ministry of proclaiming the Gospel, of leading people in intercessory prayer and of service within, and beyond, the liturgical arena.

These practicalities may provide the focus for the applied outworking of a deacon's ministry in the liturgy, but it is undergirded by a call to embody what the Church is called to be: as God's servant in the world and to reflect the self-emptying nature of Christ reflected in the New Testament (e.g. Mark 10.43–45; Phil. 2.5–8). Consequently, it is a ministry that calls for attentiveness to others, rather than oneself; for turning away from one's own need for recognition and acknowledging the need to recognize the glory of God; for enabling relationships to be formed and questions to be asked, rather than defining strategy and direction. Significantly, the two words used in both New Testament and classical Greek, from which the title of deacon is derived, emphasize this in ways which are insightful for exercising this ministry in the Eucharist. *Diakon* is often used to refer to the carrying out of a mandated task on behalf of someone in authority, whether of an unskilled nature (such as waiting at table or clearing the vessels after a meal), or something involving considerable responsibility (such as making a proclamation on behalf of the person in authority). *Doulos* is often used to describe bond-servants and particularly those slaves who pulled the oars on the bottom rung of a ship with the clear inference of everyone pulling in the same direction.

Traditionally, the deacon has not only prepared the altar for the Eucharistic celebration and tidied up what remains before taking it to the sick and housebound later; she or he has also proclaimed the Gospel and preached the word. The deacon will also prepare the congregation for the Prayers of Penitence, for the Prayers of Intercession, and invites them to share the Peace as well as dismissing them at the conclusion of the liturgy.

The liturgical comportment of a deacon (whether that ministry is permanent and distinctive, or exercised by someone who also presides at the liturgy on other occasions) calls for an attitude of serving both the liturgical celebration and those who worship at it. Experience suggests that diaconal ministry is exercised appropriately when there is no sense of competing for the same space as the person presiding; and where movement and gestures are expressed in a way that does not distract from the ambiance being set by the president. The deacon does not simply duplicate gestures that are distinctive to the presidential role (e.g. the bold welcoming and greetings gestures), but characterizes a self-effacing restraint, as well as being attentive to the needs of the congregation. This calls, specifically, for a heightened awareness of the movements of others and a willingness to accommodate one's own movements accordingly. The oft-caricatured perception of the deacon or assisting minister who is unable to walk alongside other ministers at the same pace in processions or who believes it is their task to 'instruct' or 'correct' the president or even misappropriates the distinctive presidential functions and gestures, is completely at odds with the underlying theology of a liturgical ministry which is fundamentally concerned with enabling others to fulfil their particular calling.

A deacon should always strive not to need their own copy of the liturgy so that their hands are free and ready to assist the president (by holding the president's book, for example; or to pass things when standing beside the president at the altar). Their eyes should not be focused on their own copy of the liturgical text, but always looking towards the needs of the president and the worshipping community they are serving. It is a ministry which is prepared to do all the 'running around' (without causing distraction), so that the president can be still and focused. This, inevitably, calls for a much greater degree of behind-the-scenes preparation, of being prepared to commit the basic shape, words and movements of the liturgy to memory. This is just a hint of how the dynamic of service and sacrifice come together in the way this ministry is exercised in the public liturgical arena.

It is worth remembering that the gestures and comportment of all who exercise a liturgical ministry, whether as deacons or lay ministers, contributes to the overall impact of how an act of worship is experienced by the entire worshipping community. Because the body language of all who minister at the Eucharist conveys deep meaning and significance, it must be always orientated away from self in order to point to a greater reality at the heart of the liturgy – and the cosmos. As Don Saliers has identified:

> Ritual activity is . . . concerned with . . . the coming of the kingdom . . . [it is] a parabolic type of activity (which throws us aside), metaphorical (which takes us somewhere else), allegorical (which speaks of something else) and symbolic (which brings together and makes connections). (1994, p. 32)

Having considered the body language and gestures, we now move to consider the environmental setting of the liturgy and how the president might use the space in which the liturgy is celebrated in significant ways.

5

Poetic Space: Inhabiting the Liturgical Environment

Space has always reduced me to silence. (Vallés, 2004, p. 238)

Human beings are more than souls or minds; they are profoundly shaped by material reality . . . it is [in] the valuing of place in and for itself that a drawing closer to God becomes possible, whether this be detected in a sense of divine immanence or in pulling beyond the specific context, into transcendence. (Brown, 2004, pp. 81, 160)

Christianity emerged from a Jewish world in which there was much theological investment in the significance of particular places as the location of divine disclosure and encounter. Christianity adopted this instinct, partly because, with Jews, it acknowledges God as universal creator and believes that the material world offers a means to glimpse the creative glory of the creator; but also because the incarnation of Jesus Christ bears witness to the creator being made manifest in human flesh and blood in specific locations. This belief has always been held in creative tension with the conviction that the resurrection of Jesus Christ and the outpouring of the Spirit at Pentecost has made not just certain places, but the whole earth, potentially a place of divine encounter. Added to which, Christianity has never lost the Jewish instinct for pilgrimage to particular places of significance; but it also insists that the entire cosmos is imbued with a sense of holiness without ever denying the potential for evil in the world and the human capacity to destroy God's good creation.

Consequently, Christian worship utilizes material things. The Eucharist, which uses the physical elements of bread and wine, is always celebrated in a specific physical space. Christian worship takes place in a particular cultural, historical and spatial environment, and the liturgical president is called to enact the words and gestures of the liturgy in relation to that space. It could be a small orthodox church crammed in among the houses of a narrow street in a Lebanese or Egyptian city, in one of the earliest places to receive the Christian mission: almost-anonymous outside; its internal spaces richly ornamented with icons; the air a heady fusion of incense and the smells of the streets outside; the whole perspective irradiated by the candles which are a sign of the prayers of the faithful. It could be a hall in a school – or community centre – at the heart of a post-war English housing development, which lacks any obvious Christian symbolism; where the liturgical furniture is assembled for worship on a Sunday and packed away for the rest of the week. Or it could be an awe-inspiring Gothic cathedral at the centre of an historic European city, where the intricacy and detail of the original architecture and furnishings almost require a lifetime's attention; where subsequent generations have added furnishing and ornamentation which reflect an evolving artistic and theological perspective.

Whatever the space and wherever its location, it will have a significant bearing on the way the Eucharist is shaped and celebrated. Its constraints and opportunities will impinge on how a worshipping community expresses its understanding of itself in the liturgy. More especially, the words, the gestures and the movements of the president take place in these spaces in relation to this physical environment. The worshipping arena will have a significant bearing on the way those who worship are enabled to participate in the drama of the liturgical action at many different levels. As has been observed in previous chapters, just as the function of the brain can have an impact on the employment of language, music and movement of the body (see especially Chapters 3 and 4), so it can have a bearing on the way we understand and absorb the significance of space. Our memory of places and what takes place within them mutates and feeds our expectations.

The French philosopher, Gaston Bachelard, has written of how our initial impressions of home can profoundly shape the way the human imagination functions in different spaces, with his suggestion that the spaces we inhabit (particularly from an early age) transcend their purely physical and geometrical dimensions. He emphasizes the importance of our first childhood home as a kind of cosmos, whose shape informs our perception and experience of other 'cosmoses' long after we have left or outgrown it. For example, cupboards and drawers invite enquiry and discovery of what has, so far, remained unseen; ascending stairs (initially viewed from below) hold out the possibility of immensities beyond us, in the same way a vast forest or ocean might; while small recesses and niches feed our capacity to value the significance of the miniature, for accepting solitude, for being able to exist in something as small as a shell. In other words, our most impressionable perceptions of space can open up the possibility of 'worlds within worlds'. As Bachelard expresses it:

> One feels that there is *something else* to be expressed besides what is offered for objective expression. What should be expressed in hidden grandeur, depth. And so far from indulging in prolixity of expression, or losing oneself in the detail of light and shade, one feels that one is in the presence of an 'essential' impression seeking expression . . . that one is in the presence of . . . immediate immensity . . . (1958/64, p. 186)

Such insights are significant in understanding how the spaces in which Christian worship takes place have evolved and how we interpret and utilize them now – not least because our present cultural disposition tends to view buildings and spaces in largely utilitarian terms. However, more ancient societies invested all spaces, whether domestic, educational, civic or ecclesiastical, with a degree of significance. This informed the beliefs and life-style of those who inhabited them, as well as expressing their experience and understanding of the world.

A cursory historic survey of the spaces used for worship by Christians (as well as their religious precursors) demonstrates this inclination to give expression to belief by physical, geographical and geometrical placing. Places of prayer and pilgrimage can be found in remote high places (e.g. Croagh Patrick in Ireland, Mount Athos in Greece, or the Chapel of Saint-Michel d'Aiguilhe near Le Puy in France) which express something of the human desire to come closer to the limitlessness of God the creator, who dwells not only in inaccessible places but, as Moses discovered (e.g. Exod. 18), is enshrouded by the mystery of the clouds. Such places speak of the otherness of God, who seems beyond our immediate grasp, who invites (even compels) us to rise above the familiar world of the everyday, to contemplate the reality of the divine in strange and unexplored places. By contrast, many places of worship are located, or have their origins, in caves (e.g. the Church of the Nativity in Bethlehem, the Grotto of the 'Black Virgin' of Rocamadour in France, the crypt chapel of St Wilfrid at Ripon Minster in North Yorkshire – the cave over which the present Cathedral was developed). These spaces suggest wombs or tombs, an inward movement: to face the darkness, perhaps; or to make that interior journey suggested by the labyrinth found in the floor of many medieval cathedrals (one has been incorporated into the newly laid floor in the nave of Wakefield Cathedral, for example). They suggest pilgrimage (especially by the tantalizing suggestion of what might lie beyond the darkness) but also birth and resurrection. Alongside caves and the high places, there are wells and pools (e.g. Walsingham in Norfolk) which evoke the sources of life and faith, invite refreshment and renewal and allude to the vocation of all the baptized; and significant Christian personalities (e.g. Cuthbert of Lindisfarne) acknowledged the importance of the sea and rivers as places of prayer and encounter with the divine.

By acknowledging the different dimensions of distinctive spaces, I want to suggest that they might call for different approaches to the way words are spoken, levels of language are employed, bodily gestures enacted, symbols deployed, and how people perform within them. I also want to suggest that different spaces enable something fundamental about the nature of the Church and the community gathered for worship to be expressed within them. All liturgical space is, in the words of the French liturgist Louis-Marie Chauvet, an 'informed' space: it speaks before any words are spoken within it.

Complexity and Accessibility

A Sunday celebration in a spacious medieval church, which invites further exploration beyond what can be seen or comprehended in a single glance, which contains intricate carving in stone and wood, rich colouration in the glass and where complex music may accompany the liturgy, calls for what David Brown has described as 'a richness in language and action that allows worshippers to explore and be explored by a Being who is beyond all possible containment' (2004, p. 20). In such a setting, making the liturgy 'accessible' (in the narrowly defined sense of having its language and symbols explained and defined to such an extent that further exploration is discouraged) would be to create a dissonance between the content of the liturgy and the environment in which it is celebrated. The challenge is to discern how 'contemporary' elements introduced into such an environment might develop and enhance, not clash with, the spatial surroundings.

For example, because most medieval churches are much larger than the size of the population they were originally built to serve, in order to accommodate processions and other dramatic acts, the liturgy might reflect this by including movement to different spaces within the building to punctuate particular moments of the rite. This need not necessarily be restricted to those exercising a liturgical ministry: all worshippers might be given the opportunity to do this (e.g. finding a different space, with a different symbolic focus, to pray after receiving communion; or moving with the liturgical ministers at the end of the liturgy to the place of blessing and dismissal).

A smaller, less elaborate environment, such as a weekday celebration in the side chapel of a multi-purpose suburban church, built in the 1960s, which is shared by Anglican and Free Church worshippers, might provide a more 'direct' space. It implies clarity and simplicity, demands less intricate ceremonial, provides a greater focus on the congregation gathered in one place to hear the word and celebrate the sacrament and suggests that more 'concrete' and pictorial language will be appropriate in a space that is devoid of many other visual elements. The challenge is to understand how the architecture's emphasis on immanence – the contemporary world and the presence of Christ in the midst of *this* local community gathered for worship – might be expressed in worship which resourcefully introduces an added sense of the transcendent which is not in conflict with the tenor of the architecture. How might the gestures of the president, as well as the words and music, enable a congregation to imagine what is not physically present? Certainly, language that triggers the imagination and invites silence will be helpful in such a context; as will music of a direct character which is easily appropriated, whether it is one of the simpler Gregorian chants, a metrical Psalm, Taizé chant or a worship song.

Both examples encourage worshippers and president to ask to what degree are our worship spaces predominantly vertical or horizontal: to what degree does the worship offered in them provide a balance between the immanent and the transcendent; immediacy as well as depth and height? Does the space encourage you to look up or look within; does it evoke wonder at the vastness of creation or the smallness of the womb and the tomb?

These are questions with which every Christian community and every liturgical president must wrestle because much of the worship that is currently encountered in the Church of England, today, often suggests that little account is being taken of its spatial setting. Worshipping communities and liturgical presidents do not instinctively ask how a particular space might potentially enhance what worshippers will receive from the liturgy; how it might more effectively communicate the theology which underpins the liturgy; or how worshippers might express their belonging to the Church with greater insight and authenticity.

It must be admitted that most buildings for worship in the Church of England have inherited an architectural style that was either imposed on earlier buildings during the Victorian era, or has subsequently influenced peoples' perceptions and memories of what a church is 'like'. Fixed and inflexible wall-to-wall pews, with very little space for liturgical movement in the main body of the church, with worshippers focused on a fixed (and often cramped) 'sanctuary' which assumed a didactic model of discourse from the clergy to the congregation, have created a dissonance between the form and content of worship and the space in which it takes place. Such constraints are hardly encouraging liturgical presidents and worshippers to invest theological and aesthetic significance in the building where the liturgy is celebrated. And yet, where the architectural and spatial perspective is, at best, of secondary significance, it is bound to have a constraining effect on a priest's capacity to preside with insight and imagination.

The residual ambivalence towards the spatial setting of the liturgy is explained only in part by the Church of England's architectural heritage. Equally significant are the influences which shaped our liturgical origins in the wake of the Reformation as well as the subsequent cultural and historical momentum which has accompanied the development of Anglican worship (see pp. 22–3). A suspicion of the physical and symbolic, a preference for the functional over the beautiful, and a rejection of the visual as a means of mediating the divine, has resulted in a clear division between proclamation and manifestation. For worshipper and president alike, meaning has become dislocated from the environment and ambience in which it is spoken or enacted. The ethical is championed over the aesthetic.

This is but a hint of the ambivalence that has always existed in the Judeo-Christian tradition towards architectural symbolism in general and figurative art in particular, epitomized by the debate over icons in the eighth century and the destruction of images in many churches during the Reformation in the sixteenth century. As David Brown has stressed, the presuppositions of the Reformation remained remarkably resilient in supporting a culture of rationality, where theology has reflected an approach of 'valuing the arts not in their own right but only in so far as they "preach the gospel"' (2004, p. 22).

This stance has persisted into the late twentieth and early twenty-first centuries. For example, when Basil Spence's original proposals for the new Coventry Cathedral (consecrated in 1961) contained plans which not only took account of developing liturgical scholarship at the time, but also looked back to the design of the Byzantine basilica, such as Ravenna begun in the mid-sixth century, his proposal was opposed by clergy and others who favoured a more familiar layout. It prompted the then Provost of the new Cathedral to comment, 'whether they were Gothic or tin shanties, the essential purpose of a cathedral could be proved in any context' (Spence, 1962, pp. 41ff).

Similarly, the American Methodist scholar, Susan White, has argued that the material–spiritual divide has been most keenly felt among post-Enlightenment Protestants. Although this is being increasingly challenged by a recovery of the biblical roots of a theology of place, where the importance of land, temple and pilgrimage is given substantial emphasis, White also argues that what makes particular spaces 'sacred' is not self-evident or self-perpetuating. Rather, the meaning of a particular place is dependent both on the degree of significance that people are willing to attribute to it and on the ethical values enacted within it. The beauty of a place of worship, or the testimony of an encounter with the divine in the past, does not necessarily constitute the sacredness of a particular place – now or in the future (Brown and Loades, 1995, pp. 32ff).

Both examples demonstrate the pervasive influence of a theology which suggests that it is *people* that make places 'sacred', not the location itself. Significantly, in relation to Coventry's design, it was the 'outsider' who challenged the Church with an aesthetic perspective which invited a reconsideration of existing architectural, theological and liturgical perceptions. Coventry's decision to opt for a basic layout, which reflected the pervasive instinct for what a church should be 'like', not only reflected some of the insights of Bachelard (see p. 134), but drew critical reaction from both architect and theatre director:

> The ultimate causes of the Church of England's failure to cre-ate a living architecture are theological rather than architec-tural. They stem from the Church's failure to think out afresh its own function and that of the *domus ecclesiae* in a post-Christian society . . . So long as we continue to consider the problem of the modern church as being primarily an architec-tural one, to be debated in an aesthetic vacuum, we shall come no nearer to finding a solution . . . (Hammond, 1961, p. 11)

> there is a new building, fine ideas, beautiful glass-work – only the ritual is threadbare. Those Ancient and Modern hymns, charming perhaps in a little country church, those numbers on the wall, those dog-collars and the lessons – they are sadly inadequate here. The new place cries out for a new ceremony, but of course it is the new ceremony that should have come first – it is the ceremony in all its meanings that should have dictated the shape of the place, as it did when all the great mosques and cathedrals and temples were built. Goodwill, sincerity, reverence, belief in culture are not quite enough: the outer form can only take on real authority if the ceremony has equal authority . . . (Brook, 1968, p. 53)

As I hope to illustrate below (see p. 147), there are aspects of Coventry's architecture which offer a favourable theologi-cal perspective in comparison to other buildings of the same period. Nonetheless, Peter Brook's observation, in particular, points to particular challenges and opportunities which have been grasped elsewhere. For example, Salisbury Cathedral

(1220–58) was conceived around the liturgical choreography which would take place within it; just as the Anglican Cathedral at Portsmouth (completed in 1986) was a much older building primarily reordered in recent decades to accommodate the Easter Vigil liturgy.

If a liturgical celebration is to be cohesive and unified, it needs be 'at home' in its surroundings. The relationship of worship to its physical surroundings may be complex, but it is also vital in reflecting the multi-dimensional nature of what is taking place in every celebration of the Eucharist. This comes as a salutary reminder when the pace of liturgical renewal and revision has been unprecedented in recent decades, but the substance of this activity has been concerned with the composition of texts, with comparatively little emphasis given to the question of *where* worship will take place and *how* it might be enacted in particular places. Very often, it feels as if we are expecting people to come to worship with little expectation that the environment might be as transforming as the words which are spoken or sung.

Examples of Contrasting Shapes and Purpose

The Chapel of King's College, Cambridge (begun in 1446) is one of the world's iconic religious buildings. Its architecture represents the apotheosis of European Gothic flamboyance – and some of its geometrical patterning has been clearly influenced by the Muslim cultures encountered on the crusades. Its superbly conserved medieval glass, in which Old and New Testament narratives are presented in allegorical pairings to reflect the prevailing mode of biblical exegesis of the time, is the finest of its kind in the world. Its choir is a world-class exemplar of musical excellence. It primarily serves a distinguished, multi-disciplinary academic community which belongs to an otherwise 'secular' institution. It is also a magnet for many visitors and tourists for whom worship in the Chapel is a once-in-a-lifetime experience. The liturgical language employed is predominantly drawn from the Book of Common Prayer and the Authorized Version of the Bible. The music which intertwines with the spoken word represents the very best of each historical period, where intricate polyphony from the sixteenth century is an obvious reflection of the architecture and history of the building, but the angular, exigent pallet of many contemporary works seeks to reflect the social and cultural milieu with which present-day worshippers must engage. The liturgical language deliberately invites enquiry and reflection, just as its architecture and furnishings demand sustained visual attention. The musical repertoire deliberately avoids the less enduring examples of the English choral repertoire and gives primary emphasis to music which voices an historical, cultural and theological catholicity, which makes intellectual and artistic demands of those who hear it – and perform it. The visual impact of the Chapel, in which stone, glass, wood and (especially in winter) candlelight disclose many different levels of symbolism, draws the eye towards the Eucharistic action at one end of the building beneath the great East window with its illustration of the passion of Christ and Rubens' *Adoration of the Magi*, which depict the two central dramas of salvation. This is no 'ordinary' space, and what takes place within it, linguistically, musically and symbolically, necessarily communicates in a nuanced timbre.[1]

The pilgrimage church of Notre Dame de Haut in Ronchamp, Eastern France, is the work of the celebrated Swiss architect Le Corbusier (1887–1965), completed in 1954. It dates from the architect's so-called 'brutalist' period. Its interior is a space of stark simplicity, lacking in ornamentation, with a random, almost chaotic, approach to the placing of the windows and the distribution of light. Its gradient, sloping floor provides fixed seating of theatre-like dimensions, with the attention of the worshipper being inexorably drawn to the sanctuary. The internal dimensions, seating and liturgical furniture, create a strong sense of being firmly rooted, and the organic nature of

---

1 See www.kings.cam.ac.uk/chapel/index.html.

the structure has often been compared to a mushroom emerging from the earth. It appears to anticipate the liturgical emphases which would characterize the Second Vatican Council. If the interior seems to express contemporary immanence, the exterior, with its towers pointing above and beyond the roof of the main church, invites a consideration of possibilities beyond this world. This is a building that not only draws pilgrims and visitors, it is also home to a religious community. The combination of immanence and transcendence in the architecture is matched by a fusion of transience and stability among those who worship in its spaces. Here, the contemporary Roman rite, with its emphasis on simplicity, seems entirely at home and the minimalist nature of the liturgical choreography seems all of a piece with its architectural surroundings.[2]

Vertical and Horizontal

In Chapter 2, consideration was given to aspects of the historical roots of the Eucharist, its development and how an understanding of this history might be reflected in the manner of the president today. Of particular concern was the question of whether the liturgical consciousness of the earliest Christians was shaped by the paradigm of temple or synagogue. As I hinted at the conclusion of that chapter, this discussion is also pertinent to the physical worshipping environment and how a priest presides at the Eucharist in different buildings with different visual and symbolic emphases.

Very often, the impression given is that the rite and the building in which that rite is celebrated do not always cohere. This is because the space and the way that space is understood and interpreted can result in a one-dimensional impact. The

---

2 See www.fondationlecorbusier.fr/corbuweb/morpheus.aspx?sysId= 13&IrisObjectId=5147&sysLanguage=en-en&itemPos=3&itemCount= 5&sysParentName=Home&sysParentId=11 and www.collinenotredame duhaut.com.

contemporary, immanent components are often given significant emphasis in the texts, spoken and sung, which value the
horizontal dimensions of worship; but less attention is given to
expressing the vertical aspects, where movement in the building and the architectural features of the building itself provide
height and depth and point to realities beyond this world. In
spatial terms, it is possible to see how an unquestioned assumption that the synagogue provided a model for the origins of
Christian worship was translated into the development of one-
dimensional, even functional, liturgical space.

The synagogue was as much a place of education and, particularly for diaspora Jewish communities, a social and cultural
space, as it was a centre for worship. The essence of much synagogue design, as far as the 'prayer hall' is concerned, tends
towards fixed seating focused on and often orientated around a
raised platform on which there is a table for the reading of the
Tor'ah (the *bim'ah*), a prayer desk or pulpi, and the Ark (*Aron
Ko'desh*) or cabinet that contains the scrolls of the *Tor'ah*.
Such an arrangement will be familiar to many Christians and
resembles much post-Reformation church design. It is a basic
layout found in Quaker meeting houses, for example, as well
as church buildings which have been influenced by the inheri-
tors of the European Reformers such as Calvin. The iconic
European examples are Amsterdam's Nieuwe Kerk, St Peter's
Cathedral in Geneva and the Grossmünster in Zurich.[3]

It is also an approach that can be found in a modern Roman
Catholic Cathedral. Frederick Gibberd's Metropolitan Cathedral of Christ the King in Liverpool was begun in 1954, less
than a decade before the opening of the Second Vatican Council.[4] This was also a period when many Roman Catholic theologians who were influential in the liturgical reforms of the
Roman Catholic Church during the 1950s and 60s, such as
Josef Jungmann and Yves Congar, were beginning to accept

---

3 See www.nieuwekerk.nl/en/; http://www.saintpierre-geneve.ch/ and
www.grossmuenster.ch/.

4 See www.liverpoolmetrocathedral.org.uk/.

some of the Protestant critiques of pre-Reformation Roman Catholic practice, and this tendency has clearly influenced the liturgical design of the building.

Church as 'Synagogue'

Gibberd's cathedral at Liverpool reflects the synagogue paradigm. It is, essentially, a building in which worshipers gather in fixed seating, in circular formation, around the altar and ambo (or lectern) to hear the word proclaimed and celebrate the sacraments. It speaks of God in the here-and-now, where a sense of a particular community gathered around a central worshipping space is inescapable.

It speaks uncompromisingly of a God who is encountered from within the community's worship, where an awareness of the contemporary world and those with whom we worship is underscored by the architecture and the way the liturgy is celebrated in relation to its physical surroundings. This is the Church expressing itself as the body of Christ, gathered to break bread around the table of Lord. This mode of worship 'in the round' conveys what it means to belong to the fellowship of faith after being admitted through baptism. The worshipping environment is confined to one space, and there is little suggestion that much lies beyond it. It provides worship which is instinctively on the 'horizontal plane': earthed and incarnational in character. This is not simply a reflection of the liturgical principles of the Second Vatican Council (see p. 49), it also echoes the practice of some European reformers in the sixteenth century, notably Martin Bucer, who encouraged a circular configuration around the preacher. This pattern may have influenced Thomas Cranmer and the English reformers, following the 1552 revision of the Book of Common Prayer, where those receiving communion were called into the chancel of the church and would kneel around a long table before receiving the communion elements from vessels which were similar to domestic cups and plates.

This worshipping environment advocates a model of the Church and a liturgical pattern which can prove attractive to those seeking the securities and solidarities of a well-defined community or family. However, circles can be difficult to penetrate, especially if you are unfamiliar with the worshipping life of the Church; if you are unsure how your life and experience complement those who already belong to the circle; or you find it difficult to locate the point of entry. Also, circles are usually orientated inwards. This can result in a liturgical pattern which is time-specific and anthropocentric: a community of the like-minded not easily challenged by or accommodating of other perspectives. This has significant implications for the Church's missionary bearing towards its wider context: first, because circular liturgical configurations can easily give the impression that newcomers and seekers are welcome insofar as they conform to the norms and expectations of the existing community; and second, because circles tend to invite worshippers to turn their backs towards those who are outside.

As David Stancliffe has perceptively acknowledged, the principal weakness of the Liverpool configuration is that it implicitly makes the Eucharist the static terminus of the building, with all other sacramental celebrations (e.g. baptism) isolated at the periphery. The circular arrangement of the central worship space also demonstrates how difficult it is to give equal emphasis to word and sacrament in this space (with a proportion of the congregation situated behind the person speaking at the lectern) or to give expression to the linear movement from word to sacrament, or the relationship of the Eucharist to baptism (Stancliffe, 2008, p. 256). How, for example, did the architect envisage the liturgy of the hours (the choral offices of Morning and Evening Prayer) being celebrated in that same space or the liturgy of Good Friday which invites worshippers to make a 'pilgrimage' to venerate the cross?

The limitation of the 'synagogue' paradigm is relatively easy to diagnose. The challenge lies in discerning how the celebration of the liturgy in such a space can be ordered to address some of the more obvious disadvantages, while also embracing

some of the opportunities that might more naturally lend themselves to a 'temple' setting – without creating the sense that
the liturgy is in conflict with the shape and momentum of that
space.

Church as 'Temple'

It was noted earlier how, in his design for Coventry Cathedral
(1961), Basil Spence had initially attempted to reflect 'current'
theological and liturgical emphases in his design (see p. 140).[5]
His intentions were obstructed by those for whom the 'Gothic'
configuration of a church was more familiar – not least because
most English parish churches underwent restoration in the late
nineteenth century, in schemes heavily informed by the impressions of medieval architecture and liturgical practice espoused
by J. M. Neale and the Cambridge Camden Society, for example. What resulted at Coventry, which has frequently been dismissed as England's latest Gothic cathedral, nonetheless offers
worshippers a more wide-ranging experience of the liturgy than
the 'circular' configuration of a church such as Liverpool Metropolitan Cathedral – not least by its suggestion that there is a
vertical as well as horizontal perspective to the building and the
worship offered within it. This happens in a number of ways.

First, although the 'new' cathedral is undoubtedly a twentieth-
century creation, worshippers enter it either through, or close
to, the ruins of its medieval precursor. A sense that the building
has a past and has been shaped by decisive historic events is
inescapable. There is a clear implication that Christian worship
and the celebration of the Eucharist in particular invites the
worshipper to engage with the past as well as the present and
the future. There is a physical suggestion of memories of past
events. As Mary Collins acknowledges, '[l]iturgical Worship
commemorates the past proclamations of God in human living

---

5 See www.historiccoventry.co.uk/cathedrals/newcathedral.php.

as well as makes one sensitive to those that will enter at some future time' (1987, p. 80).

Second, on entering the building worshippers are drawn forward. The eye – as well as the body – is invited to move beyond what is initially encountered. Their focus and perspective shifts as they progress through the building. There are hints of other places, which invite rest or contemplation or engagement, which can be found by 'turning off' the main route – to the Chapel of Unity and the Baptistery, for example. As the worshipper is drawn closer to the high altar, which is the focus of the building, it becomes apparent that it is not a terminus: beyond it are other spaces such as the Lady Chapel and the Chapel of Christ the Servant. Alongside this sense of forward movement is a clear suggestion that there is more, still awaiting discovery, at different levels. This is especially evident if the worshipper has been walking forward through the building towards the high altar and then looks back from where they began, to see (probably for the first time) the ten stained-glass windows which are orientated to project light towards the altar.

Third, the iconic presence of Graham Sutherland's great tapestry of 'Christ in Majesty' seems to accompany every stage of movement through the building. The immensity of the figure of Christ (particularly in proportion to the human figure who stands dwarfed between his wounded feet), his posture and the deliberate modelling of the figure on the classical Byzantine images of Christ, speaks powerfully of his otherness. It challenges any sense that the worship offered in the Cathedral is merely an expression of the contemporary community's perspective. Although the brief that invited architects to compete for the commission to design the Cathedral spoke of the altar as the 'people's altar', the presence of the figure of Christ tells us that it is *his* altar too and his sacrifice on the cross which we recall and celebrate there: we cannot simply possess it as our own. In the words of one perceptive interpreter, 'The sacred has been defined as that to which we have access but which is not at our disposal' (Mayne, 1998, p. 19). The symbols of the four evangelists, with their bestial representations surrounding

Christ, add to this sense of being confronted by an unlikeness to the world we already know. It inspires worshippers and those who preside at the liturgy to acknowledge that Christian faith and worship has its roots in other times, other places and other ways of perceiving reality.

Coventry is comparable to the Temple in providing many contrasting spaces at different levels. Both Jerusalem temples had interior and exterior courts, gathering spaces, chambers at different levels and, in the first Temple, figurative art. It was a sacred space where pilgrims and worshippers were not given immediate access to the Holy of Holies (or a place near to it), but were required to make a patient journey over the various thresholds in a place where worship was as much about sights and smells, prophetic utterance and glimpsing the mercy seat of *Yahweh* as it was about the reading and interpretation of scripture. Coventry Cathedral is a building in which worshippers are given time and space to participate in its worship by different degrees. This is a model of the Church as a pilgrim people, of seekers and enquirers being encouraged to progress at their own pace, to cross thresholds and experience new landscapes. The building does not yield up its secrets and treasures as soon as access is gained. No one is being compelled to join the circle, neither does it suggest that people must conform to someone else's notion of what Christian community means. Worshippers can linger at the back, or find a distant space elsewhere in the building. It is possible to loiter, wonder, reflect and give attention to the creative insights of others. And yet, such a church is not without its prophetic dimension. Pilgrimage through this building will bring the worshipper face to face not only with a vast representation of Christ in glory, who calls, judges, forgives and heals, but also with the challenge explicit in the Cathedral's ministry of international reconciliation (expressed by the Chapel of Unity), with the suffering of the human race (in the Gethsemane Chapel with its striking 'Angel of the Agony' mosaic and crown of thorns) and the juxtaposition of the Church's worship with the demands of daily life and work in the Chapel of Christ the Servant, where the everyday human transactions on Priory Street provide a backdrop to worship in this space.

Something of this 'pilgrimage' pattern, of being taken out of the familiar and being led to an encounter (to use Auden's striking expression) 'in the land of unlikeness', has been observed in some examples of 'Alternative Worship'. These (predominantly) Church of England initiatives offer 'alternative' liturgies aimed at those who feel themselves unable to belong to 'traditional' churches. For example, York Minster's *Transcendence* Eucharist begins in the Minster's Chapter House (configured in the round in an octagonal space). However, before the Gospel is heard, worshippers are invited to follow the book of the Gospels in a movement from the Chapter House into the Minster itself.

> The procession had something of the atmosphere of going on pilgrimage, the book of the Gospels carried at our head, with the sense that we followed Christ. The movement and the walking together singing had the mood of approach to the holy place, in this case the holy place being not so much the arrival in the Minster nave as the encounter with Christ who, having gone before us, was waiting to welcome us, perhaps transform us . . . (Perham and Gray-Reeves, 2011, p. 47)

The vast majority of those who are called to preside at the Eucharist will do so in much smaller and possibly more constrained spaces than Liverpool or Coventry Cathedrals. Similarly, it is very easy to provide a straightforward contrast between two architectural styles and not acknowledge that, both historically and contemporarily, the situation is less polarized than might superficially appear. Any consideration of the history of the development of Christian architecture will recognize that the synagogue model has influenced the temple pattern and vice versa. For example, the Syrian liturgy before the fourth century, with its strong linguistic and symbolic temple associations, nonetheless made the *Bema* (or lectern) for the proclamation of the word a focal point of its churches. Today, many celebrations of the Eucharist take place in Norman or Gothic buildings, with the temple paradigm explicit in their design, but where the underlying theological and ecclesiological tenor of the liturgy emphasizes that the locus of the sacred is the community gathered around the Lord's Table. Nonetheless, it is hoped that, by taking time to contrast the two basic styles, Eucharistic presidents will be encouraged to ask some elementary questions about the church buildings in which they currently lead worship.

- Is the paradigm of your building, predominantly, that of synagogue or temple? What model of the Church does it reflect?
- To what degree does the architecture, the configuration of the worship space and the style of worship offered allow a balance of vertical and horizontal? At what point do sacred space and the wider world meet?
- Where do you place the emphasis on your ministry as a Eucharistic president: as host at the family meal table; as teacher; as priest in the temple; as conductor of an orchestra; as one encouraging the pilgrim community to move towards new goals and horizons?
- How can those entering this space and participating in the liturgy be invited to experience what they see and hear from a new perspective?
- How are these emphases and opportunities reflected by the way you 'inhabit' the particular worshipping space in which you preside?

By giving serious consideration to the architectural and artistic environment of the liturgy, it is possible to recognize that liturgy itself is an art form, with many layers of expression and meaning. There are high and low points, hard and soft features, loud and quite moments, light and dark features, all of which contribute to the overall shape and structure of the Eucharistic action. Giving serious consideration to the space in which the Eucharistic celebration takes place will enable the president to make informed choices about how their words and actions relate to that space, to enable those who worship to sense that their own participation is not restricted to what they hear or say – or even read from a page. It also happens as much with what they see, smell, reflect on from memory and imagination and how they sense themselves in relation to God and the rest of the Church, how they are lifted out of themselves, within a particular space. As one poet has recognized (and in which it is possible to read a suggestive allusion to the cruciform shape of many church buildings and the cross as the tree of life):

> Space, outside ourselves, invades and ravishes things:
> If you want to achieve the existence of a tree,
> Invest it with inner space, this space
> That has its being in you. Surround it with compulsions,
> It knows no bounds, and only really becomes a tree
> if it takes its place in the heart of your renunciation.
>
> (Rilke, cited in Bachelard, 1958, p. 200)

Alongside these reflective questions are the applied implications of how the layout and furnishings of a particular worshipping space can articulate the theology implicit in the rite and enable the emphases of transcendence and immanence, of pilgrimage and community, to be underscored in diverse spaces.

Furnishing Essentials

A Sedentary Calling: The Presidential Chair

It has already been noted that, as early as the second half of the first century AD, Justin Martyr identified the one authorized to oversee the celebration of the Eucharist as the 'president', and this is a term that persisted over the course of subsequent centuries. To preside means, by definition, to 'sit before', and the deliberate placing of the Presidential Chair was a feature of certain patterns of church architecture in the earliest centuries, notably in the classical basilicas.[6] During the Middle Ages and the period following the Reformation, it was a piece of furniture which became obscured by the central focus of altar and pulpit; but was given renewed significance by the reforms of the Second Vatican Council with their desire to reflect earlier practices.

In many Anglican churches, today, the Presidential Chair is often overlooked: either by being placed in a restricted space (very often the 'stall' or reading desk from which the offices of Morning and Evening Prayer are more appropriately conducted) or because it appears as if it is just one among many other seats being occupied by all liturgical ministers. It is possible to discern an underlying embarrassment or unease on the part of many presidents, who mistakenly equate visible presidency with dominating the celebration. There is a tendency to resort to the language of collaboration, of a desire to enable others to fulfil a liturgical ministry, of not wanting to impede the gifts and calling of others. These are all healthy aspirations. However, only one priest (or bishop) can preside, and confident presidency will always be concerned with enabling everyone present to be fully active participants in the liturgical action, without diminishing the visible responsibility of the one who presides.

When the president has a visible and distinctive place from which to preside, it gives the correct degree of significance to those elements of the rite which are most appropriately performed from the chair. For example, there needs to be a strong sense of gathering at the start of the liturgy, which appropriately expresses the calling and dignity of those who have gathered to celebrate the Eucharist, where they are assuredly greeted in the name of Christ. Similarly, a confident and visible president is able to pronounce words and perform gestures of significance, which greet, bless and absolve, in an unimpeded manner. Viewed in this way, the Presidential Chair becomes identified as the location from which worshippers are invited to voice their praise as well as their sorrow, to be assured of forgiveness, to be

---

6 For example, San Clemente, Rome; Poreč Cathedral, Croatia; Torcello Cathedral near Venice.

drawn into the prayer of the whole Church. It is also becoming more common for the concluding elements of the Eucharist to take place at the Presidential Chair (Post-Communion Prayer, Blessing and Dismissal), and this gives the president, as well as the Presidential Chair, a vital missiological focus by being the place from which worshippers are blessed and sent out into the world, strengthened by word and sacrament.

The Word Made Flesh: The Lectern, Ambo or Pulpit

In many Anglican churches, particularly those that were re-ordered during (or following) the Victorian period, two items of furniture tend to stand like sentries at the entry to the chancel: the pulpit on one side; the lectern on the other. One is the place from which the scriptures are read; the other is the place from which the scriptures are interpreted. One is a space which all who exercise a liturgical ministry may occupy to read from the Bible; the other is space usually occupied only by those who are authorized to preach. Superficially, a clear separation between the words of scripture and the words of the preacher is being symbolized. However, the relationship of scripture to sermon has been much more complex and diverse throughout Christian history. Many of the Protestant Reformers, for example, held that the reading of scripture and preaching together constituted the Word of God.[7] Theologians closer to our own time, who have been shaped by the Reformation's heritage, reflect this conviction. Karl Barth famously gave equal weight to a threefold expression of the word of God in proclamation (the reading of scripture), preaching and revelation.[8] It has been traditional in the worship of the Free Churches, for example, to preface the reading of scripture *and* the sermon with the summons 'Hear the word of God' which is an echo of John Calvin's

---

7 For example, Heinrich Bullinger in the Second Helvetic Confession 'The preaching of the word of God is the Word of God'.

8 Barth, 1953, p. 121 sees this threefold pattern as analogous to the Trinity.

contention that 'when a man has climbed up into the pulpit . . . it is [so] that God may speak to us by the mouth of a man' (cited in Parker, 1992, p. 24). Such insights begin to question whether the reading of scripture and preaching should, physically and symbolically, be in two separate locations.

From a different perspective, the architecture of churches dating from the early centuries of Christian history, particularly in the East, suggest that where the theological perspective was very different from that of the Reformers there was nonetheless one place for the proclamation and interpretation of scripture. Following the pattern of the synagogue, there was a raised platform on which a pulpit or lectern-like structure was placed. It was a place both of proclamation and interpretation and also a place for leading the prayers of the faithful. Cyprian of Carthage, writing in the middle of the third century, provides one of the first instances of the ambo as a raised area in a Christian place of worship, suggesting that it must have been a relatively substantial feature of the worship space. This reflects something of how the 'synagogue' and 'temple' models co-existed alongside the evolution of the shape of the Eucharist, as the design of churches evolved in the early Christian centuries from smaller, domestic environments to larger, public arenas.

More especially these examples demonstrate an understanding of the significance of the proclamation of the word in relation to the celebration of the sacrament. Just as there is a place for the president to 'sit before' those who are led in worship, so the design of the ambo became more than a functional place to read the scriptures: it became a seat (or throne) on which to place the book of the Gospels as an icon of Christ (or to proclaim the resurrection at Easter through the singing of the *Exsultet* – the ancient Easter proclamation). This is reflected in the increasingly elaborate design for these structures, such as in San Clemente, Rome or Santa Maria del Lago, Moscufo.[9]

---

9 Both examples demonstrate the degree to which the design of the ambo not only became more elaborate but required its own distinctive spatial environment within the church building.

Similarly, until the late sixteenth century, the ambo or pulpit was rarely a terminus, but a place from which the focus of the liturgy moved on, to express its crucial momentum as it progressed from word to sacrament.

'The Brittle Miracle of the Bread':[10] The Sacrificial Table

As the shape of the Christian Eucharist became largely established and settled as a movement from word to sacrament, the spaces which housed its celebration required a table-like structure on which the president and worshipping community offered their gifts in response to the generosity of God. It became the focus of the celebration where they gave thanks and from which they were nourished and sustained by the life of Christ in the sacrament.

Initially, there is a strong suggestion that the wooden tables used for this purpose, such as those depicted in the frescoes in the Roman catacombs, existed well into the post-Constantinian period. At first, they were differentiated, in the Christian consciousness, from the altars found in pagan temples, in time, there is evidence that, as pagan structures were appropriated and adapted to Christian use, pagan altars were re-dedicated and stone structures eventually replaced wooden ones. Many altars were built over the tombs of saints as the pagan custom of erecting a 'ciborium' or canopy over them to provide heightened significance grew. Early examples of this exist in Italy: in San Clemente in Rome and Santa Maria Assunta, Bominaco. Modern examples of employing this style can be found in the UK at St Paul's Cathedral in London, in All Saints' in Clifton, Bristol, and The Ascension in Crownhill, Plymouth.[11]

---

10 R. S. Thomas's description of the Eucharist in his poem 'The Moon in Llyn'.

11 The cited twentieth-century examples were all constructed after the Second World War and represent both a move away from 'Gothic' assumptions about church design and an interest in earlier architectural forms.

Giving the altar emphasis did not always mean that it dominated a particular liturgical space. Rather, it was a place where the Eucharistic celebration reached its climax: a place to progress to; not always the most immediate or predominating feature of a church.

The basilicas of the fourth and fifth centuries, for example, adopted a variety of positions for the altar, depending on their location and layout and what had been the principal influence on their design. There are examples of the altar being set between the Presidential Chair and the ambo; sometimes it was raised on a platform and may be screened (not necessarily in the medieval sense, but sometimes by a low wall or *cancelli*). Evidence from North Africa suggests that altars were placed in the body of the church to allow worshippers to gather on three sides. The model adopted in the Middle Ages placed the altar centrally at the far East end of the church, with the ambo (or pulpit) and Presidential Chair becoming less prominent. Many Church of England buildings, which have been re-ordered with Victorian assumptions about medieval configuration, tend to reflect this pattern. Here, the altar is placed centrally (either against the East wall or having more recently been pulled away to allow a 'westward facing' celebration), usually enclosed by altar rails, in a raised chancel area which may also contain seating for the choir; or a moveable 'nave altar' has been placed closer to the congregation, at the point where the nave and chancel meet, where it is on a visual 'level' with the pulpit and lectern.

In the early fourth century, Eusebius spoke of the altar as the 'Holy of Holies' with the suggestion that, wherever the altar was placed, the presence of the living Christ could be encountered by virtue of the sacramental action which took place there. Such a description may seem more immediately at ease with a 'temple' paradigm, but it can also help to underline its significance in spaces which tend towards a 'synagogue' model.

First, the altar should clearly occupy one of the four focal points of the liturgical space and be recognized as a destination to which there is a degree of movement after the proclamation of the word – especially if it is placed at some distance from the body of the congregation. Second, the altar should be afforded a measure of symbolic self-expression. It should be bare and empty until the moment when it is prepared for the Eucharistic Prayer, and the temptation to place a veiled chalice or other items upon it before the liturgy begins should be resisted. Third, it is the place where the bread and the cup *alone* are placed, unencumbered by other items (such as collection plates, unnecessary additional books, keys, flowers, even the president's diary!) which may detract from the altar's symbolic emphasis. Fourth, serious consideration should be given to how many ministers need to be focally central at the altar during the Eucharistic Prayer. Again, there is an understandable desire to express the collaborative nature of the ministry being exercised by different participants in the liturgy, but whether the model is that of priest at the altar or host at the table, it should always be asked whether the presence of additional personnel at the altar is enhancing or obscuring the role of the president and the symbolic focus of the altar. Should the appropriate habitat of assisting ministers more naturally incline towards the congregation as the gathering of all the baptized, for example, or be seeking greater identification with the president at the altar? Obviously, the overall size of the building, as well as the dimensions of the altar and its surrounding space, will dictate this to some degree: a lone president standing in a vast space might suggest a ministry being exercised in isolation from the rest of the body of Christ, whereas additional ministers crowded around a small altar in a restricted space may compound a sense of visual busyness (especially if the assisting ministers are unable to sustain a sense of focused stillness).

Restated Refreshment: The Font

Some of the earliest known records of Christian practice locate baptism at the Easter Vigil and, until it subsequently became common at Pentecost also, suggest that it was the only time when baptism was commonly administered. The placing of the font, therefore, became a significant decision as churches became larger public buildings. There are many examples where elaborate structures were built over them (resulting in a baptistery either within or outside the main church). Wherever it was placed, the font was always deliberately placed in relation to the other significant liturgical furnishings – precisely because it was understood as the beginning of the liturgical journey. After emerging from the waters of baptism (usually administered by immersion), the newly baptized would 'join the procession' of all the faithful in moving to the place where the word was proclaimed, the sacrament celebrated, and the bishop sat in his chair to represent the heavenly court.

As with our consideration of other items of liturgical furnishing, the reality is that many Church of England buildings, especially those that underwent restoration in the eighteenth and nineteenth centuries, do not always reflect the practice of the early Christian centuries. Very often, the font is 'tucked away' in a corner (as was the case in St Paul's Cathedral, until 2005, when it was located in the South transept until its re-setting in front of the great West doors); or hidden behind a pillar, almost to avoid being a focal feature. This is, of course, a reflection of the way in which infant baptism had become the norm in Christian societies where the sacrament was almost taken for granted at the outset of human life, and the rite became a small-scale domestic occasion attended by the priest, the godparents and the immediate family of the baptized, gathered (symbolically for their understanding of the sacrament) just inside the church door.

This raised difficulties when, in the second half of the twentieth century, the importance of baptism was being recovered, not only as a theological foundation for the Church's self-understanding, but also because the sacrament was being increasingly administered as part of the principal Sunday Eucharist. The issue of visibility was often resolved either by re-siting fonts in a visible position close to the chancel (as it has at St Mary's, Burley-in-Wharfedale, West Yorkshire); or it became fashionable to employ a smaller, temporary font in a similar position, which could be moved out of the way after the liturgy of baptism was over.

When the *CW* baptism rite was first published it was conceived alongside the presumption that, as English society became more secular in nature, the number of infant baptisms would reduce, and there would be a correlative growth in the numbers of committed adults being baptized.[12] The rich symbolism and language of the rite sought to recover echoes and reflections of the practice of the early church. It envisaged that the rite would be celebrated less frequently in parishes and would become more of a celebration for adults coming to faith and for children from committed church families. While this has proved to be a false assumption, with the numbers of non-church families requesting baptism for their children remaining steady across the Church of England as a whole, there has continued to be a strong emphasis on the Church as the community of the baptized, with a particular emphasis on baptism as the foundational sacrament for all Christian ministry and mission.

This suggests that the importance of the font as a fundamental – and visually central – piece of liturgical furniture needs to be recovered. It should be the first item encountered on entering a church, situated in a place which demonstrates a clear connection and continuity with the altar, lectern and Presidential Chair. The font should be situated where clear symbolic emphasis can be attached to it in the liturgy (e.g. where the liturgical ministers, at least, can process to it and gather around it, if not the whole congregation). It should also be a 'working' item, and any attempt to reduce it to an ornamental article should be strongly resisted. It should be open, and its water (blessed either at a recent baptism or at the Easter liturgy) should be available to use. Worshippers should be encouraged to sign themselves with the water as a

---

12 At the time of writing, the Church of England House of Bishops is being asked to consider alternative texts for the baptism rite, especially the Decision and Prayer over the Water, which are deemed to be more 'accessible' for occasional worshippers and those for whom the language and symbolism of the rite are deemed to be culturally alien.

reminder of their own baptismal calling as well as the authority their baptism has conferred on them to be those who bear the light of Christ to the world, as they enter or leave the church. At significant feast days with strong baptismal associations (Easter, Pentecost, Baptism of Christ, etc.) it should be one of the key foci of the liturgical action. Even in those churches where 'catholic' symbolism tends not to be used, serious consideration should be given to the value of sprinkling baptismal water on the whole congregation (echoing the symbolism of Ezek. 36) as a concrete reminder of where our Christian life began and what it continues to demand of us now and in the future.

Colour

It is beyond the scope of this book to consider the architectural and aesthetic minutiae of church design. Nonetheless, liturgical presidents who are sensitive to the environment in which they lead worship will be aware of the impact of different visual dimensions on what worshippers will encounter and receive.

One obvious dimension is colour – and the changes of colour that may take place during the course of the year. Different colours in church send subliminal signals which act as visual reflections of words spoken and music sung. Colour also expresses mood and allows different emotions and sentiments to be articulated in a non-verbal manner. Iain McGilchrist suggests that the perception of colour belongs to the right hemisphere of the brain, which allows us to receive the spontaneous and implicit: allowing for the inferred and implied expression of meaning before it is analysed and defined by the brain's left hemisphere (2009, p. 63).

The use of colour in the liturgical arena and the evolving and changing use of colour can induce different impressions and sentiments (of praise, lament, penitence, joy, etc.); it can also trigger an intuitive 'reading' of the liturgical environment. To walk into a church in the Northern hemisphere in mid-December and encounter the dark hues of purple or blue, for example, can evoke feelings and suggest meanings very different from a late spring afternoon that is punctuated by the bright tones of white and gold. This is a reflection of the way colours evolve and change in the external environment, as the greens and yellows of summer foliage develop into the reds and browns of autumn, with the suggestion that where life was once abundant, it ends in death and decay, before renewal and rebirth after winter. A world without colour would be disorientating, static even, intimating a halt in growth and evolution. The presence of colour – as well as any visual art in the liturgical arena – is another means of articulating how the mysteries of faith are expressed and experienced as part of the cycle of time. It allows faith to be intuitive as well as rational; dynamic as well as stable. For, as George Herbert knew

> Doctrine and life, colours and light, in one
> When they combine and mingle, bring
> A strong regard and aw: but speech alone
> Doth vanish like a flaring thing,
> And in the eare, not conscience ring.
>
> ('The Windows', Herbert)

A final point about colour is that the normative liturgical colour scheme, broadly adopted by the Western Church today, emerged from the sixteenth-century Counter-Reformation and was prescribed by the Roman Catholic Church after the Council of Trent (1563) in an attempt to achieve uniformity. This was ably implemented by the growth in Catholic missionary orders. It is, in essence, the *Common Worship* colour scheme, which assumes white (or gold) for festivals, violet for Advent and Lent, red for Palm Sunday, Good Friday and Pentecost as well as the feasts of martyrs and green for the rest of the year. Prior to this, the medieval church had a much more diverse approach to liturgical colouring, with different churches adopting the customs of different cathedrals. When Lichfield Cathedral devised the first English liturgical colour scheme in the mid-thirteenth century, for example, it designated black for Advent; whereas Wells used blue, with Salisbury using red. Only in Exeter in the fourteenth century does evidence exist to support the wearing of purple in Advent. Similarly, bleached linen (to suggest no colour) was more widespread in England during Lent before the Reformation – not least because purple (as the most expensive dye) was more associated with luxury than penitence in the medieval mind.

Having an awareness of the diversity of liturgical colour schemes may help presidents and their worshipping communities to view the use of liturgical colour schemes in a less prescriptive light. For while a measure of commonality helps to express a measure of catholicity in worship, colour does not always seem to have been the litmus test of this quality. Consequently, account should be taken of the architecture of the church, the quality of the light at particular times of the year, the surrounding topography, as well as reference to any pre-Reformation insights.

A Place of Epiphany

In conclusion, consideration needs to be given to the degree to which the liturgical environment should differ from the familiar, everyday, domestic environment. A church is the arena of encounter with the living God and a place where worshippers may encounter what Evelyn Waugh described as 'the operation of divine grace on a group of diverse but closely connected characters' (1948, frontispiece). It suggests that the liturgical environment should be quite unlike other places where human transactions take place: not remote from the world; more a place that enables the world to be seen in a different light because of the transforming activity which takes place within it. It should be a place where epiphany is always possible, as well as a place where human solidarity is cherished and celebrated in a way that is distinct from any other social gathering. It should be distinguishable as a place where the human and divine interact, as well as being large enough to embrace the chaos of sin and hurt which people bring with them into the arena of worship,

to allow worshippers space to see themselves afresh in the light of God's transforming life.

As well as giving prominence to the main elements of liturgical furniture (see above, p. 152) and setting them in proper spatial perspective, it is vital not to confuse the significance and meaning of the liturgical arena as 'set apart' space. To make a place of worship look like any other familiar, domestic environment is to distort its distinctive purpose. As John V. Taylor identified, a place that is set apart for worship provides 'a permanent and much-needed reminder that this is not a human-centred universe: it revolves around God and for God' (1995). Consequently, allowing the introduction of items such as carpets, curtains and cushions, which are associated with places of relaxation in the home, seems inappropriate; as does their capacity to stifle resonance and the sense that sounds and voices are heard differently in the liturgical arena.

Empty Potential

In 1998 the medieval Parish Church of St Brandon in Brancepeth, just outside Durham, was gutted by fire and its notable interior, supervised by Bishop John Cosin in the mid-seventeenth century, completely destroyed (see Sadgrove, 2013, pp. 194–7).

The scale of the destruction made restoration of the original interior impossible and a catastrophe was soon grasped as an opportunity. Martin Stancliffe who, at the time, was Surveyor to the Fabric at St Paul's Cathedral, was the appointed architect. Presented with the blank canvass of an empty shell, he conceived the church (as many medieval churches were originally intended to be) as a processional space, from West to East in line with the momentum of the building, with three symbolic 'pools' of liturgical action along the way: font, lectern and altar. Additionally, there was a plan to provide an additional place for the reservation of the sacrament at the East end of the church which, so far, has not been realized. It allowed for the possibility of 'stational' liturgy where, in certain circumstances, the whole congregation progress from West to East, from font to altar, as the liturgy evolved from gathering, to proclamation of the word, to celebration of the sacrament.

The liturgical furniture, as well as the seating for clergy and congregation, was designed to be moveable (to allow use of the church for other events such as concerts or drama); but the stone floor was designed in such a way that the place of the font, lectern and altar were clearly defined and marked out. This emphasizes that, although the items may be removed for 'secular' occasions, their presence – and significance – is still distinguished in the floor patterning. They are, somehow, non-negotiable 'presences' in the building which, even when physically removed, still leave the trace of their location in the ground, as they chart the journey from word to sacrament, from earth to heaven.

Liturgical presidency is always much more than the reading of the right words, performing the right actions, wearing the right clothes, singing the right notes, standing or sitting in the right place. Fundamentally, it is about orientating oneself and those who are being led in worship towards the mysterious reality of God in our midst. The building in which the liturgy is celebrated is a vital dimension in enabling this divine reality to be sensed. If it is deemed to be much more than just another functional space and invites worshippers to consider themselves standing on the threshold of another world, it may also sharpen their perception of what the world at large could become when they are sent back to it from transforming activity of participating in the liturgy. The space where the liturgy is celebrated should always be orientated in such a way that the human mind and heart is confronted by a beauty which is not of human origin, which not only surprises but also endures. As the German architect, Rudolph Schwarz, has identified:

> A meaning is stored up even in that building which is nothing more than an instrument and thus in it, too, the rapidly passing process is embedded in a lastingness which speaks into the building from its remoteness. (1938, p. 79)

6

Practising the Scales of Rejoicing: Shaping a Liturgical and Presidential Instinct

> . . . the Spirit must practise his scales of rejoicing
> . . . and the Soul endure
> A silence . . .
>
> (Auden, *For the Time Being*, 1944)

- How do you discern how to preside well at the Eucharist?
- How do you sustain and develop the impulse that enables you to grow as a liturgical president?
- How do you use your voice, body, memory and imagination to enable the whole people of God to grow through worship?

A musical analogy may help to probe these questions.

Learning to play a musical instrument requires the student to absorb basic rudimentary techniques which, once mastered, will facilitate the performance of more complex music. A first piano lesson, for example, will begin with locating 'middle C' on the keyboard and becoming familiar with the other notes in relation to it. This leads to various exercises – arpeggios and scales especially – which will enable the player to commit to 'muscle memory' the fundamental technique necessary for playing much of that instrument's repertoire. It also requires certain physical postures: the positioning of the fingers above the keyboard, the body's poise when seated at the keyboard, the proximity of the body to the instrument, etc. Basic rhythms are learnt, followed by syncopation which makes rhythm more complex; as is an ability to give music an expressive quality through volume and phrasing. A small child embarking on her first piano lessons may protest at having to 'practise scales' every day, but will soon realize that, without this disciplined attention to the basics, it will become impossible to master the sonatas of Mozart, the waltzes of Chopin or the preludes and fugues of Shostakovich; nor will she succeed in mastering more complex instruments, such as the organ or harpsichord, which depend on the foundational techniques first mastered at the piano.

As every musician also knows, it is vital to maintain these early disciplines if the standard of performance is to be maintained and developed. It is not simply a matter of reaching the required standard in order to obtain certain qualifications and, having obtained them, adopt a dismissive or careless attitude to the rudimentary disciplines of the instrument.

As I know to my cost (and sometimes embarrassment!), the music I was able to play 15 and more years ago, because I was playing the organ regularly before training for ordination, I would now struggle to give convincing performances of. This is simply because I have allowed the regular physical and mental habits associated with organ playing to drop: creating time to rehearse the fundamentals regularly, imaginatively interpreting the intentions of the composer (which may involve keeping up with emerging scholarship about methods of performance in various historical periods), even remembering to adopt the physical and mental attitudes required to play convincingly (the position of the fingers, the positioning of the body on the organ stool to enable both hands and feet to negotiate the full compass of the key and pedal boards, etc.). I might 'get away with it' (in terms of playing the notes in the right sequence, with mistakes along the way), but I would hardly inspire my listeners or offer them new insights about the piece I am playing. Similar analogies could be employed from the experience of scientific enquiry, participating in a team or individual sport, dramatic or other artistic endeavours. Very similar dynamics and disciplines are also at play when it comes to presiding at the Church's liturgy.

In this concluding chapter, I am attempting to offer from my own experience and from the insights of others, a range of habits, disciplines, tendencies and inclinations which may prove helpful in nourishing the life of all who are called to preside at the Eucharist. Far from being a systematic (or fail-safe) 'spirituality' for effective and imaginative presidency, this is a collection of pointers that I have found valuable as I have struggled to grow in this vocation. My hope is that, having shared these insights, they may encourage others to develop a pattern and rhythm which sustains this ministry.

Worship

It may seem excessively obvious to begin with this observation, but unless a president is able to worship, they are unlikely to be able to lead others in worship. Those who lead others towards a vision of the triune God can only do so if they have themselves first been inspired (and continue to be inspired) by such a vision in the liturgical arena. If I believe, from lived experience, that worship can both enlarge and transform, I stand a better chance of persuading others that this is so. When worship is flat and one-dimensional, it is often rooted in an inner ambivalence about its transformational potential by those who preside at it. Unless the president's foundational conviction is that presiding at the Eucharist is what makes their ministry distinctive, there will remain a lingering uncertainty about the value and significance of their role, as well as hesitancy concerning this crucial dimension of worship as a means of envisioning the kingdom of God.

This is where the reality of exercising a liturgical ministry is anchored, and Tim Gorringe has suggested that the dullness which characterizes much worship is a sign not so much of sloppy preaching or poor preparation (which undoubtedly contributes to it), but also of a tendency to 'retreat from the depths rather than face them' (Gorringe, 1997, p. 85). This voices Gorringe's concern that, in worship, there is always a temptation to retreat into cloying superficiality because our natural inclinations as worshippers is a complex intermingling of hunger for reality and flight from reality. Moreover, 'reality' is made up of moments of passionate intensity as well as the more mundane dimensions of life. Tribal genocide in Rwanda and 9/11 may be 'reality' but, as the parables of Jesus demonstrate, so is a woman sweeping a room or a group of men loitering in the market place looking for work. Worship enables us to see both the routine and the remarkable with heightened sensitivity. Consequently, those who create space in their lives to worship not only develop a heightened sensitivity towards the many ways in which the ordinary can become extraordinary; those who lead others in worship, particularly by presiding at the Eucharist, also express how the words and gestures of the rite can reflect the 'real world' – both here and in the eternity of which the Eucharist is a foretaste. As Gorringe puts it, 'celebrating the sharing of bread . . . recalls those who have no bread to share' (p. 86).

Being able to worship enables the liturgical president to feel at home in the 'sanctuary' where, in the words of Michael Sadgrove, we are 'given access . . . to God's way of seeing things' and a '. . . transformed understanding of the world' (2008, p. 97). If the liturgical president has high expectations of worship's transformational potential, as well as viewing the leadership of worship as the summit of their calling, it can be a decisive means of countering the lack of expectation (not to say the frequent boredom) with which many people approach the liturgy. It is also the first step in undermining the monotony that lacklustre worship can generate, so brilliantly expressed by W. H. Auden's prayer:

O God, put away justice and truth for we cannot understand and do not want them. Eternity would bore us dreadfully. Leave thy heavens and come down . . . Become our uncle. Look after baby. Amuse grandfather. Help Willy with his homework. Introduce Muriel to a handsome naval officer. Be interesting and weak like us and we will love you as we love ourselves. (*For The Time Being*, 1944)

The capacity to worship is the antidote to the contemporary obsession with self-interest and self-promotion, and those whose worship is orientated towards the living God may find they embody a kind of passive resistance to a restricted and self-referential world-view. By opening our eyes to perceive new realities beyond ourselves, worship allows us to plumb the depths of life and reach out to grasp its heights. Not for nothing has the experience of worship often been likened to a relationship of love, of affirming an 'other' as life's centre of gravity. Rowan Williams memorably described such a bearing as being 'the moment of acknowledged conviction, shared by two people, that each is accepted, given time and room, treated not as an object of desire alone, but as a focus of fascination and attention' (2000, p. 155). That is a long way from a transactional or utilitarian view of life, where 'usefulness' becomes the prevailing criterion for establishing worth or value in others; but it is just a hint of how presidents can evoke, both in themselves and in others, a capacity for worship which is a need (whether recognized or not) in all human beings. If a president is able to grasp this and convey it to others, it can become crucial in exemplifying how worship is the foundation of a renewed vision of reality:

> We must rediscover for ourselves within this culture the Christian vision of God . . . Even in our privatised culture, people still seek moments and places to celebrate a sense of human solidarity . . . The challenge . . . is to show how [a] vision of God may contribute powerfully to the desire to find communion with others, express compassion for others, and transform the world. (Sheldrake, 1998, p. 202)

Cultivating Attentive Silence

The physical, mental, spiritual and emotional demands which presiding at the liturgy extract can be considerable, which is why it is essential for presidents to discover where their 'still centre' can be found. This can often be the most effective way of being restored and refreshed – as well as facilitating proper preparation for the act of presiding. The liturgical president who is incessantly busy before services, visibly and audibly talking to servers and musicians as worshippers arrive, obsessively flitting back and forth between the sanctuary and the vestry, arriving late, not being settled before the liturgy begins, can be the most potent factor in counteracting the transformative impact of worship. A casual approach to the task, which allows a president to arrive with barely time to spare before the start of the liturgy, is an all-too-accurate reflection of an ecclesial culture which has been content to diminish the significance of liturgical presidency. A president can only commend the value of silence to those they lead in worship if worshippers have first glimpsed in the president a capacity for stillness, as someone who can create silent 'pools of reflection' by their presence and bearing alone, which allows words, music, symbols and colours to be absorbed as part of a more enlarging experience. As R. S. Thomas observed, this is an aspect of divine encounter which both demands and rewards:

> I pray and incur
> silence. Some take that silence
> for refusal.
>   I feel the power
> that, invisible, catches me
> by the sleeve . . .
>   I know its way with me;
> how it enters my life,
>   is present rather
> before I perceive it . . .
>   ('The Presence', 1984, p. 152)

It is a substantial test of presidential creativity to maintain a silent presence both before and during the liturgy – and to do this while maintaining a sense of celebration and welcome, without appearing to be stand-offish, disengagedly pious or downright miserable! The pressures to collude with all kinds of displacement activity (joining in an atmosphere of superficial bonhomie in the vestry, not challenging a culture of 'busyness' in church, where gossip and the business of committees and councils jostle in the ten minutes before the start of the liturgy, consenting to an ethos where it is commonplace to 'have a quick word' with people before worship, when it could wait until later) should not be underestimated. If a president believes that they are preparing to celebrate and embody the mystery at the heart of the Church and that what they are about to do is of supreme significance, they must convey to others that they believe it to be of supreme importance. As Sam Wells observed, silence can be a potent

> reminder that God works while we sleep, and so is a permission to those who meet you to rest. It will be an embrace of those qualities and those gifts in those around you that others have been too busy or too threatened or too self-absorbed to see and encourage. It will be an invitation into a place of depth, but an exhilarating invitation because it is depth without fear, depth as an adventure in which one is expecting to be met by God. It will be a place and a time of renewal where others rediscover who they are and who God is. And it can be almost all of these things without you ever saying one word. This is the power of silence. If you haven't discovered this power, I fear that all the words in the world or the prayer book may not be able to help you. But if you have learned this power, and learn to enjoy it as the power of God, then you have found the secret of the heart of God . . . in silence God may speak and act or God may not. But if you have met God in the sound of an echoing silence, you will never be alone. (Unpublished lecture, 2012)

Similarly, during worship it is relatively easy to displace opportunities for silence by resorting to the superficial. Moments that demand an intensity of silence (e.g. in preparation for corporate confession, in preparing to say the Collect, after the congregation's consenting 'Amen' at the conclusion of the Eucharistic Prayer as they contemplate the consecrated elements, or after receiving communion) can be often dislodged by a preoccupation with the notices or the invitation to coffee afterwards, irritation that the children are making too much noise in another part of the church, or a simple failure to recognize that the Eucharist is not simply just another communitarian activity but takes us to the threshold of eternity. In practical terms, expectation can be heightened and a congregation's experience of worship significantly enhanced if the start of the liturgy emerges out of silence rather than the usual organ-music-covered chatter. Creating the space five minutes before the start of worship in order to welcome the congregation, deal with any essential notices, followed by an invitation to keep silence (and having the confidence to hold that silence for at least two minutes) before the opening hymn is announced and sung should become a fixed part of the pre-service routine. It will also enable the president to immediately follow the hymn with a liturgical greeting and firmly establish the tone and tempo of the worship.

Above all, Baron von Hügel's advice to his niece to be 'silent about great things' should permeate deep into the consciousness of those who preside; as should his view that we should resist the temptation to discuss or explain these great things superficially instead of keeping silence before them because 'discussion is so limiting and distracting. It makes things grow smaller. You think you swallow things when they ought to swallow you . . .' (von Hügel, 2001, p. 16)

Embodying Paradox

The consideration of silence highlights the degree to which contemporary liturgical presidents are products of a cultural momentum which depends on language and is determined by language as the basis of establishing reality. However, those who lead others in worship are called not so much to define and delineate by language and action, but to embody contrasts, contradictions and opposites, as they invite others to glimpse unexpected and unforeseen realities. In other words, they are called to bear witness to something of the paradox found at the heart of worship and the Christian life, where heaven and earth, material and spiritual, explicit and implicit, visible and invisible, speech and silence, consonance and dissonance are held in creative tension. Presiding at the liturgy is rarely an absolutely 'either/or' enterprise – rather, it constantly seeks to open up new vistas and encourage the holding together of seeming opposites.

I was recently told about a diocesan bishop who began the liturgy of blessing the oils on Maundy Thursday in his cathedral by insisting he would not be 'blessing' the oils to be used in baptism and confirmation, in ministry to the sick and in ordination, because he did not 'bless' inanimate objects. While this may appear to be a reductionist view of the potential of divine activity in the material world, reflecting a view of rationality flowing from a post-Enlightenment world-view, it also highlights a surprising lack of confidence in the paradoxical dimensions of worship. As Iain McGilchrist has recognized:

> The Western Church has . . . been active in undermining itself . . . [and] joins the chorus of voices attributing material answers to spiritual problems. At the same time the liturgical reform movement, as always convinced that religious truths can be literally stated, has largely eroded and in some cases completely destroyed the power of metaphorical language and ritual to convey the numinous. Meanwhile, there has been, as expected, a parallel movement towards the possible rehabilitation of religious practices as *utility*. (2009, p. 441)

If worship is to be much more than a quantifiable and calculable activity, it requires those who preside to engender in those they lead in worship what Aidan Kavanagh famously called a 'liturgical seeing'. This stems from the conviction that liturgical insights are not simply formed in the mind and intellect of the person presiding alone; they become evident and tangible in the corporate, ritual activity of the whole Church. This not only sounds a cautionary note to those who seek to suggest that a given ritual act can be invested with a sole symbolic meaning or expresses a specific doctrinal norm; it also invites president and worshippers to explore and discover how doctrinal formulations are shaped over time through participation in the liturgy, because the experience of worship can be an arena for the development of belief and tradition. Having a generous and healthy sense of the paradoxical will alleviate the temptation to make too hurried a transition from what Paul Bradshaw has called 'description to prescription' – in other words, to impose one-dimensional meanings. In the liturgy, private and public meanings collide with ancient and modern insights, cultural and theological perspectives, normative and exceptional viewpoints; and liturgical presidents are called to be sufficiently secure, theologically, to be able to embody the tradition they have inherited while also being imaginative interpreters of other insights which might illuminate and enlarge 'received' understandings. Bradshaw illustrates this point with reference to the 1552 Book of Common Prayer. Those with an awareness of the historical circumstances in which this revision came to published, as well as the theological stance of those responsible for its composition, would conclude that it was intended to give liturgical expression to a significantly 'low' doctrine of the sacrament. Nonetheless a considerable number of leading Anglican divines in the seventeenth century were able to convince themselves that a much 'higher' sacramental doctrine could be read out of the rite, and it continued to be interpreted in that way by significant personalities in the centuries which followed (Bradshaw, 1998). A delight in paradox liberates us from being confined to a one-dimensional world.

A Singing Voice

In the Orthodox churches it is a requirement that those who are to be ordained should possess a singing voice of sufficient quality with which to preside at the liturgy. This is because Orthodox liturgy articulates and expresses the faith and the prayer of the Church in song. Following the practice of Judaism, music is the vehicle for prayer, praise and lament in the Church's sacrifice of praise. It is also an indication of the degree to which the celebration of the liturgy forms the bedrock of the ecclesial, theological and ministerial identity of those churches.

This is a dimension of formation for ministry which is, largely, overlooked in Anglican training institutions. Those who feel diffident or insecure about their ability to sing tend to be allowed to continue to indulge their phobia – simply because other ministerial skills are deemed to be of greater use or importance. However, encouraging ordinands and serving clergy to sing confidently will enable them to bring a distinctive dimension to bear on the worship at which they preside. It will not only facilitate an added sensory 'texture' to the liturgy, it will widen the potential for prayer, praise, lament and penitence. I can recall two fellow students with whom I trained for ordination who were, initially, fearful of the sound of their singing voices: one now serves in an independent school where choral worship (at which he sings) is broadcast from time to time; and the other, now serving in a cathedral, is undertaking one of the singing awards administered by the Royal School of Church Music. Examples of such persistence are, sadly, rare among those preparing for ordination or among serving clergy. Where it has happened, it has invariably strengthened good working relationships between clergy and musicians – and that can only have a positive impact on the overall quality of worship! More vitally, it has allowed a president to introduce a dimension of difference to the liturgy, which invariably invites worshippers to engage at an unexpected level.

Western Christianity, as it has developed particularly in the wake of the Reformation, has not always regarded music as fundamental or necessary. This is another pointer to the way in which the brain's left hemisphere has been enabled to dominate the right's preference for the affective and implicit in aspects of the development of Anglican liturgy. Much of the dismantling of the complexity of the medieval liturgy in post-Reformation Europe was exemplified by differing attitudes towards the place and significance of music – especially its relationship to the spoken word. With the exception of the more radical Puritan sects, however, the Reformers seemed to understand the significance of music, not only as an instrument by which a new theological and liturgical ethos might be established, but also because music (however much it had been simplified in the light of what had preceded it) was valued as a means to extend and amplify the meaning of the word. The French, Swiss and Scottish metrical psalm-tunes, which typified the Calvinist legacy, were echoed in Germany and Scandinavia by the Lutheran Chorale (a medium which was to receive its most sophisticated treatment at the hands of J. S. Bach nearly two centuries later). Eighteenth-century English Methodism is said to have been 'born in song', and its founders, John and Charles Wesley, produced over 6,000 hymns between them, many acquiring a foundational place in the Christian formation way beyond the Methodist Church. More recent Evangelical and Charismatic movements have formed their identity around particular styles of music and composers, with many of their worship songs now finding an assured place alongside more classical hymnody. Nonetheless, many of these developments have valued music insofar as it enables words and meanings to be imparted and interpreted, rather than encouraging the enjoyment of music purely for its own sake. However, the two current principal growth areas in the Church of England already identified (cathedrals and charismatic congregations) are contexts where music is employed to heighten and punctuate the drama of worship, to give implicit and suggestive liturgical emphasis, as well as appeal to the non-rational. As the American philosopher Suzanne Langer has suggested, music can induce within us 'emotions and moods we have not felt, passions we did not know before' (1942, p. 222, also cited in McGilchrist, 2009), which points to its capacity to amplify the human emotional vocabulary. In short, the capacity to sing can lead worshippers to new frontiers.

The ability to sing in the liturgy also provides a physical link with elements of our past history and those formative periods of Christian development. It is significant that the foundation of Western music is plainsong: the primitive chant of Christian worship. Investing the time and energy to sing the traditional plainsong at the start of the Eucharistic Prayer, for example, is one way of introducing a heightened dimension of the intuitive and the 'other' to worship that might otherwise be too 'rational' in its aural register. For example, when I began working in my current parish, I introduced the practice of the president singing the plainsong introductory dialogue and preface to the Eucharistic Prayer (which is something I had always done throughout my ministry). There was an acknowledgement by worshippers that this not only gave the words a strange resonance, that it introduced to a 'contemporary' liturgy an element of the 'primal' (as someone asked if that is how Christians would have prayed this prayer in the early centuries of our history), and it also created a focused stillness as people's mental 'receptors' seemed to re-tune to a different sensory experience. My own experience of singing this part of liturgy is that, because it requires a different level of concentration and breath control, it creates a different intensity of physical and mental awareness within me which impacts on others in unexpected ways. As Dietrich Bonhoeffer recognized:

> It is the voice of the Church that is heard in singing together. It is not you that sings, it is the Church that is singing, and you, as a member of the Church, may share in its song. Thus all singing together . . . must serve to widen our spiritual horizons, make us see our little company as a member of the great Christian Church on earth, and help us willingly and gladly to join our singing, be it feeble or good, to the song of the Church. (Bonhoeffer, 1954, p. 45)

The capacity of plainsong to evoke a sense of the 'other' is evidenced by its popularity in the 'classical charts' (recordings by the Spanish monks of San Domingo sold over six million copies when they were signed up by EMI in the 1990s). Similarly, Jeremy Davies has movingly told of his ministry to a dying priest by singing plainsong; its lack of bar lines and metrical pattering providing an almost timeless, floating quality which points beyond the ordered rationality of this world. While the American jazz historian, Ted Gioia, has written about the adverse impact of removing plainsong from the liturgy of a monastic community, following the reforms of Vatican II. He describes how monks, who had been able to thrive on little sleep, became tired, irritated and lethargic when the chanting of plainsong was removed from their daily liturgical rhythm. They became more susceptible to infection and illness. Only when one doctor recommended the re-introduction of plainsong was their equilibrium restored, as they returned to their praying, their reliance on short periods of sleep and their original pattern of work. A change in soundscape had profound consequences for individual well-being and community flourishing. (Gioia, 2006, pp. 100ff). As Aidan Kavanagh has noted, if something is worth celebrating, it is worth singing about (1982/90, p. 31).

Again and Again . . .

Presiding at the Eucharist, though always a unique and fresh undertaking each time it takes place, is always a repetitive activity. This repetition creates its own rhythm and momentum, which anchors both president and worshippers in an evolving and developing tradition, as they find themselves 'picking-up' the tempo and cadence of worship which has pulsated through the Church's life from the very beginning. Again, Orthodox worship bears witness to this. The text of the liturgy is unchanging, and even the music to which that text is set, or the liturgical choreography of the ministers, may not vary considerably from one celebration to another. However, it would be myopic to conclude that this mode of worship is static. Not only is it undergirded by the conviction that, each time the liturgy is celebrated, the whole cosmos is renewed; but what president and worshippers bring to the celebration each time will be different from the week before, as will the gifts and blessings they receive from it. This is a welcome perspective when presidents face many pressures which can undermine their confidence in this repetitive rhythmic pattern; when the contemporary cultural fear of boredom, as well as the insatiable ecclesial obsession with liturgical novelty, seems all-pervasive (see p. 76).

Being at home in this repetitive and rhythmic liturgical pattern is a necessary dimension of effective presidency. Repetition, coupled to the evolving and alternating rhythm of the rite, creates its own impetus which can liberate presidents from a reliance on the printed page. Having a keen sense of the shape of the liturgy and the moments when the pace quickens or slows down will enable presidents to establish a rhythmic pace, to maintain momentum and avoid the feeling of 'going over speed humps' which happens when meaningless gaps occur between parts of the liturgy which should more naturally flow from one to the next. In that sense, presiding becomes akin to being the conductor of a symphony, where the text of the liturgy provides the basic 'script' (or score) but requires insight and sensitivity to know when to introduce silence between 'movements' or when to introduce an element of rhythmic elasticity ('rubato' in musical language), so that worshippers feel they have been caught up in a liturgical momentum which has rest as well as motion, exuberant impetus as well as attentive stillness.

Repetition is also crucial to the overall formation of the president's ministry. Timothy Jenkins has accentuated the importance of being formed through small-scale repetitive and collective practices and through the disciplines that form habits in our lives. The value of this for presidents might be that, by being given time and space to repeat the presidential act over and over again (its words, gestures, music and symbols), we are gradually bringing an 'external mind' to bear, so that the goal of a president's ministry will not be so much personal achievement, but to become a channel for the Church's giving and receiving. As Jenkins has suggested, such recurring activity 'represents the possibility, and the truth, that we are not simply the sum of our egos and strivings, but are capable of extraordinarily more, and that we are ordered quite differently in that . . . the key to our lives is gift, not equivalence or calculation' (2006, p. 46).

One feature of the repetitive character of worship, which has captured the liturgical imagination of many churches over the past couple of decades, has been the distinctive tradition of singing which emerged from the ecumenical Taizé community in Burgundy (and has proved to be an archetype for similar compositions from the Iona community and for 'chants' by composers such as Margaret Rizza and Howard Goodall). This particular method has been likened to a musical form of reciting the 'Jesus Prayer', where the same phrase or melodic shape is repeated to allow it to take hold at a deeper level of consciousness. Not unexpectedly, the Orthodox theologian Olivier Clément recognized its intrinsic value to the whole Church:

> Something very interesting at Taizé is that this formula of calming repetition has been taken up in the liturgy; that is, it is not used only in personal prayer, but also in prayer together or common prayer. Some young people, who know almost nothing of mystery, are introduced to it here, and they begin to learn how to pray.[1]

Forming the Heart: Choosing our Companions

If presiding at the liturgy is an enlarging experience, it important for presidents to identify what influences, personalities, art forms, places and activities might accompany and shape their formation and development in this ministry. Presidents not only feed those they lead in worship through language, actions and symbols; this feeding is informed and nourished by a developing tradition to which a president is called to be open and receptive. In other words, there is a sense in which the tradition articulated in the liturgy lives on and outworks itself as the liturgical president is encouraged, challenged and inspired by others who have walked the Christian way.

Writing from an anthropological perspective, Timothy Jenkins has identified how continuing formation supports the development of a particular character, which is sustained because we share formative ways of life with others – whether

---

1 Clément at www.taize.fr/en_article338.html.

historical or in the contemporary milieu. In particular, he suggests that being formed by those who have themselves been formed by Christian tradition (and notably its scriptural substance) is a necessary element in a priest's continuing growth and development.

> [it] involves how you spend your time, and in whose company . . . By and large, one becomes a Christian because the people one takes seriously themselves take Christianity seriously . . . What sort of tradition are we formed in, that constitutes our lens for reading and applying Scripture? If we read and used imaginatively writings of people who themselves had been formed by prayer and the study of Scripture, and who had put to work what they had learnt in interpreting their world anew, we might . . . see how to create a common Christian mind in the present time. (Jenkins, 2007)

This is not simply a matter of being exposed to biblical or liturgical texts, commentaries, or theology generally, but also the work of those conspicuous cultural personalities whose creativity has been informed and shaped by the cadences of Christian tradition, of which William Shakespeare, Iris Murdoch, Palestrina, T. S. Eliot, Fra Angelico, James MacMillan, Elizabeth Jennings, Marc Chagall and Salley Vickers might be random (and eclectic!) examples. I think also of those role models in various spheres of life who have implicitly or explicitly had a bearing on my sense of vocation – either by affirming or challenging it – closely or at a distance. Whoever's company we choose to keep, such personalities can become companions, interpreters and critics, offering the liturgical president an almost infinite perspective through which to understand and exemplify the tradition he or she is called to articulate.

Equally, whoever presidents identify as formatory influences, it is important to identify also those whose company may be less obvious or attractive. The recognition in the Rule of St Benedict (Chapter 61) that strangers to the community are to be given an opportunity to comment upon, or give critical reaction to, the life of the monastery could be interpreted as accepting there may be occasions and instances where those we find least appealing can be our most effective teachers. Consequently, if my preferred reading is science fiction, I may have something to learn from literary or political biographies; if I am a scientist who deals predominantly in empirical evidence, maybe I need to listen to more music or expose myself to more art – not so much to analyse it as simply to enjoy it; if my ideal relaxation is a television soap opera, perhaps I should go to the theatre more regularly (or vice versa). The observation of R. S. Thomas about the poet's craft could be appropriately applied to any art form or human endeavour which has integrity and has the potential to open the mind and heart to the things of God:

> The nearest we approach to God, is as creative beings. The poet, by echoing the primary imagination, recreates through his work the forces of those who read him to do the same, thus bringing them nearer to the primary imagination, and so, in a way, nearer to the actual being of God as displayed in action. (1963, p. iii)

Hospitality and Feasting

At the heart of the Eucharistic celebration is a recalling and re-enacting of the self-giving of God in the death and resurrection of Jesus Christ. It bears witness to a God whose nature is revealed as generous and abundant. Moreover, the Eucharist is a foretaste of the eternal banquet which reflects our Jewish roots with its succession of feasts and the prophetic vision of all peoples, nations and languages being invited to participate. This is expressly echoed in the Gospel parables which not only speak of people being invited to a feast or banquet, but many of which were told in the context of Jesus being a guest at the tables of others. To that extent, it is not surprising that one commentator has suggested that the inclusion of these parables by the Gospel writers is an indication of the possibility that, among the first generation of Christians, fundamental issues of doctrine and ethics were deliberated, settled and worked out in the context of table fellowship and the breaking of bread (Drury, 1973, p. 88).

How presidents embody these realities is one of the privileges (as well as the demands) which undergird their ministry. As anyone who offers hospitality in the domestic arena of the home will know, it is an activity that demands time, imagination, empathy and a willingness to accept that, when a particular combination of people come together to share food, drink and conversation, the event can take on a 'life of its own' with unforeseen outcomes. This points to the need not only for thorough preparation, but also the need to cultivate a 'feel' for when it is right to create space for spontaneity. In that sense, all hospitality is open-ended: the host cannot precisely predict what the assembled company will give and receive from the encounters and interactions. This hints at the degree to which Eucharistic celebration, as well as foreshadowing the feast of God's eternal kingdom, can also be a vision of a redeemed social order in the here and now. It highlights how presidency carries fundamental pastoral and missiological assumptions, in seeking to exemplify how the quality of Christian community is tested by the willingness of a diverse mingling of humanity to sit and eat together. If presidents can see this potential in the celebration of the Eucharist, it will inform a sentience in all worshippers that the healing of personal, political, ecclesial and social wounds belongs at the heart of the Church's worship. As Sam Wells has acknowledged:

> eating together bestows on the Church its identity, because it gives it a definitive practice. Learning to perform this action well informs and educates Christians in their performance of all other actions. If the Eucharist is the definitive practice of the Church, it is the first place Christians should look to guide their own practice . . . In Eating together Christians discover what it means to be the Church. (2006, pp. 129–30)

Thankfulness

This final 'habit' is, perhaps, the most crucial of all. To preside at the Eucharist is to be a channel for the thanksgiving of the whole people of God. It is to find oneself caught up in the ceaseless offering of thankfulness and praise which has been – and will continue to be – the duty and delight of the Church until the end of time. Like the need to be formed by worship, thankfulness may seem like an obvious quality to possess. Nonetheless, the ministry of very few presidents is focused solely on liturgical leadership. Other demands, pressures, distractions, opportunities, frustrations and anxieties are an inevitable part of the ministry of most priests, whether in the parish or another sphere. We bring our hurts, betrayals, tiredness, foolishness, failures as well as our achievements and satisfactions and a whole host of other sentiments to the altar. In these circumstances, what keeps a president focused on the fundamental necessity for joyful thanksgiving in the enactment of the drama of salvation?

Similarly, the life of most church communities (and the Church as an institution) can be characterized by disagreements and tensions, despondency and malaise, as well as by individual people who are ill, grieving or depressed – and there is bound to be the odd personality (or two!) who finds that a worshipping community is a convenient arena to outwork a deep-seated and unresolved pathology. Any combination of these (and other) factors can make churches potentially thoroughly uninviting places and can impact significantly on the collective mind of a congregation. In such situations, a deeply rooted instinct for *eucharistia* is a necessary prerequisite in all who preside at the Church's defining act of worship, whose name means 'Thanksgiving', because it provides an antidote to cynicism and melancholy.

This is an insight which reaches back beyond the origins of Christianity and is particularly evident in the Psalms, where complaint, lament, the bearing of injustice and treachery, as well as the enormity of unexplained suffering, is frequently resolved in an outpouring of thanksgiving for the good things of life. Michael Sadgrove has pinpointed this dimension in his consideration of Psalm 73, where worship offers a 'shaft of illumination' in a situation overshadowed by the psalmist's envy at others and the weariness which accompanies the practice of faith. On entering the sanctuary, the Psalmist sees things in proper perspective by being confronted by the truth of God's generosity and the joy to be found in having communion with the one who is the source of all gifts and blessings (2008, p. 97).

Understood in this way, Eucharistic presidency can become an act of resistance in a cultural milieu where pessimism and contempt are all-pervasive. To embody a capacity for thanksgiving can be both shocking and surprising in situations where worshippers need to be stretched beyond their immediate vista and invited to reach out and grasp the love, the joy and the abundance which is God's endless desire for his people and the whole created order. This is where the act of liturgical celebration – for both president and worshippers – becomes truly transformational because of its potential to transfigure what motivates us at the deepest level.

Of course, this capacity for thanksgiving is not suddenly acquired, nor does it superficially assuage the aches and wounds that are present in the world as well as the Church. To celebrate the Eucharist with thanksgiving is to create a space in time where we acknowledge that love is stronger than hate and life is stronger than death. It is to be caught up in the drama of crucifixion transfigured by resurrection over and over again. This is what makes Eucharistic presidency a hopeful vocation: not because presiding anesthetizes the enormity of whatever else is going in life, but because the Eucharist holds before us a vision of what ultimately matters in life – and beyond it. This is evidenced in a story told by the Dominican priest, Timothy Radcliffe, when he came close to the pronounced trauma of ethnic genocide in Rwanda:

Everything was coming to bits, the country was on fire as we drove through this suffering land. We were pulled out of our car, machetes and pistols put at our heads. I didn't think we were going to survive the day. [We] made our way to a hospital filled with young kids who'd lost their limbs with mines. I remember one particular kid lost two legs and an arm and an eye and his father beside him weeping. And then we went back to the Dominican Sister's house filled with bullet holes from fighting the previous day and I wondered, what could I say? I couldn't think of any word I could offer. And then I remembered there was something that we could do, which is the foundation of all Christian hope. We could celebrate the Eucharist, which takes us back to that darkest night when Jesus gave us a sign of hope. So that's what gives us the courage to go forward. (1996)

When destructive forces seem overwhelming, whether in one of the world's war zones or because the agenda for the church council promises to be especially demanding later that evening, the objective character of the Eucharistic feast always holds before us a way forward – even when there seems to be none.

To amplify the point I made about worship near the beginning of this chapter, it is the dimension of thanksgiving which streams through the celebration of the Eucharist which gives it its enlarging character. Just as laughter is sometimes uncontrollable when we are spontaneously and unexpectedly delighted, so the stream of thanksgiving which irrigates the celebration of the Eucharist cannot be impeded either by whatever heartaches and vexations occupy the president and those being led in worship. Rather, the elemental trait of thanksgiving challenges us to acknowledge that there is much, much more – and that we can never rest content with the here and now. This is why 'it is right to give thanks and praise' because the liturgical president is called to bear witness that the risen life of Christ is *now*.

Bibliography

Adams, William Seth, *Shaped by Images: One Who Presides*, New York: Church Hymnal Company, 1995.

Auden, W. H., *For the Time Being: A Christmas Oratorio*, London: Faber & Faber, 1944.

Bachelard, Gaston, *La poétique de l'espace*, Paris: Presses des Universitaires de France, 1958; English translation: *The Poetics of Space*, Boston: Beacon, 1964.

Bailey, Kenneth E., *Jesus through Middle Eastern Eyes*, London: SPCK, 2008.

Baldovin, John, *The Urban Character of Christian Worship: The Origins, Development and Meaning of Stational Liturgy*, Rome: Pontifical Oriental Institute Press, 1987.

Barker, Margaret, *The Older Testament: The Survival of Themes from the Ancient Royal Cult in Sectarian Judaism and Early Christianity*, London: SPCK, 1987.

Barker, Margaret, *The Gate of Heaven: The History and Symbolism of the Temple in Jerusalem*, Edinburgh: T&T Clark, 1991.

Barker, Margaret, *The Great High Priest: The Temple Roots of Christian Liturgy*, London: Continuum, 2003.

Barker, Margaret, *Temple Themes in Christian Worship*, London: T&T Clark, 2008.

Barth, Karl, *Church Dogmatics 1.1*, Edinburgh: T&T Clark, 1953.

Billings, Alan, *Making God Possible*, London: SPCK, 2010.

Bonhoeffer, Dietrich, *Life Together*, London: SCM Press, 1954.

Bracken Long, Kimberly, *The Worshipping Body: The Art of Leading Worship*, Louisville: Westminster John Knox, 2009.

Bradshaw, Paul F., *The Search for the Origins of Christian Worship: Sources and Methods for the Study of Early Liturgy*, London: SPCK, 1992 (revised edn: 2002).

Bradshaw, Paul F., 'Difficulties in Doing Liturgical Theology', *Pacifica*, 11:2, 1998.

Bradshaw, Paul F., *Eucharistic Origins*, London: SPCK, 2004.

Bradshaw, Paul F. and Johnson, Maxwell E., *The Origins of Feasts, Fasts and Seasons in Early Christianity*, London: SPCK, 2011.

Bradshaw, Paul F. and Johnson, Maxwell E., *The Eucharistic Liturgies: Their Evolution and Interpretation*, London: SPCK, 2012.

Briggs, David, 'The Art of Improvisation', unpublished lecture given to the Incorporated Association of Organists, June 2010.

Brook, Peter, *The Empty Space*, New York: Touchstone, 1968.

Brown, David and Loades, Ann (eds), *The Sense of the Sacramental: Movement and Measure in Art and Music, Place and Time*, London: SPCK, 1995.

Brown, David and Loades, Ann (eds), *Christ: The Sacramental Word*, London: SPCK, 1996.

Brown, David, *God and Enchantment of Place: Reclaiming Human Experience*, Oxford: Oxford University Press, 2004.

Brown, David, *God and Mystery in Words: Experience through Metaphor and Drama*, Oxford: Oxford University Press, 2008.

Brown, Raymond E. and Meier, John P., *Antioch and Rome: New Testament Cradles of Catholic Christianity*, New York: Paulist Press, 1983.

Browning, Don S., *The Moral Context of Pastoral Care*, Philadelphia: Westminster, 1976.

Buber, Martin, *I and Thou*, London, Continuum, 2004.

Bultmann, Rudolf, *Theology of the New Testament*, London: SCM Press, 1952.

Chapungco, Anscar J., *Liturgies of the Future: The Process and Methods of Inculturation*, New York: Paulist Press, 1989.

Chojnaki, Stanislaw, *Ethiopian Crosses: A Cultural History and Chronology*, Milan: Skira, 2006.

Clark, Neville, *Preaching in Context: Word, Worship and the People*, Rattlesden: Kevin Mayhew, 1991.

Clark, Neville, *Pastoral Care in Context: Vision of God and Service of God*, Rattlesden: Kevin Mayhew, 1992.

Collins, Mary, *Worship: Renewal to Practice*, Washington: Pastoral Press, 1987.

Common Worship: Services and Prayers of the Church of England, London: Church House Publishing, 1997–2009.

Cross, F. L. (ed.), *St Cyril of Jerusalem's Lectures on the Christian Sacraments: The Protocatechesis and Mystagogical Catechesis*, London: SPCK, 1951.

Cross, F. L., *1 Peter: A Paschal Liturgy*, Oxford: Mowbray, 1954.

Crossan, John Dominic, *The Historical Jesus: The Life of a Mediterranean Jewish Peasant*, San Francisco: Harper, 1991.

Davie, Grace, 'A Postscript: The Place of Cathedrals in the Religious Life of Europe', in Platten, Stephen and Lewis, Christopher (eds), *Dreaming Spires? Cathedrals in a New Age*, London: SPCK, 2006.

Davies, J. G., *The Secular Use of Church Buildings*, London: SCM Press, 1968.

Davies, William D., *The Gospel and the Land: Early Christianity and Jewish Territorial Doctrine*, Berkeley: University of California Press, 1974.

De Lubac, Henri, *The Drama of Atheist Humanism*, San Francisco: Ignatius Press, 1995.

Dillard, Annie, *Teaching a Stone to Talk: Expeditions and Encounters*, New York: HarperCollins, 1982.

Dix, Gregory, *Shape of the Liturgy*, London: Dacre Press, 1945.

Drury, John, *J. B. Philips' Commentaries: Luke*, London: Fontana, 1973.

Duffy, Eamon, *The Stripping of the Altars: Traditional Religion in England 1400–1570*, New Haven: Yale University Press, 1992.

Duffy, Eamon, 'Praying in Bad Language: The Stripping of the Liturgy', *The Tablet*, 6 July 1996, pp. 882–3.

Duffy, Eamon, 'Worship', in Ford, David F., Quash, Ben and Soskice, Janet Martin (eds), *Fields of Faith: Theology and Religious Studies for the Twenty-first Century*, Cambridge: Cambridge University Press, 2005.

Dulles, Avery S. J., 'Religion and the News Media: A Theologian Reflects', *America* 171:9, 1994.

Eliot, T. S., *The Use of Poetry and the Use of Criticism*, London: Faber & Faber, 1933.

Eliot, T. S., 'Burnt Norton', *Four Quartets*, London: Faber & Faber, 1944.

Evans, Edith, 'Edith Evans', in Michael Parkinson, *Parky's People*, London: Hodder & Stoughton, 2010, p. 322.

Ford, David F., *The Shape of Living: The Spiritual Directions for Everyday Life*, London: HarperCollins, 1997.

Fortescue, Adrian, O'Connell, J. B. and Reid, Alcuin, *The Ceremonies of the Roman Rite Described*, London: Burns & Oates, 2009.

Frost, David, unpublished submission to the Church of England Liturgical Commission, 1973.

Gibbons, Robin, *House of God: House of the People of God*, London: SPCK, 2006.

Gioia, Ted, *Healing Songs*, Durham: Duke University Press, 2006.

Gordon-Taylor, Benjamin and Jones, Simon, *Celebrating the Eucharist: A Practical Guide*, London: SPCK, 2005.

Gorringe, Timothy, *The Sign of Love: Reflections on the Eucharist*, London: SPCK, 1997.

Graham, Elaine, *Transforming Practice: Pastoral Theology in an Age of Uncertainty*, London: Mowbray, 1996.

Green, Robin, *Only Connect: Worship and Liturgy from the Perspective of Pastoral Care*, London, Darton, Longman & Todd, 1987.

Griffiths, Alan, *Celebrating the Christian Year: Prayers & Resources for Sundays, Holy Days & Festivals Years A, B & C* (3 vols), Norwich: Canterbury Press, 2004.

Griffiths, Alan, *Ordo Romanus Primus: Text and Translation with Introduction and Notes*, Joint Liturgical Studies 73, Norwich: Canterbury Press, 2012.

Hammond, Peter, *Liturgy and Architecture*, New York: Columbia University Press, 1961.

Hartley, L. P., *The Go Between*, London: Hamish Hamilton, 1953.

Hauerwas, Stanley, *Hannah's Child: A Theological Memoire*, Grand Rapids: Eerdmans, 2010.

Hill, David, Parfitt, Hilary and Ash, Elizabeth, *Training Your Choir*, Buxhall: Kevin Mayhew, 2007.

Hopkins, Gerard M., *Poetical Works*, edited by Norman H. Mackenzie, Oxford: Clarendon, 1990.

Hovda, Robert, *Strong, Loving, Wise: Presiding at Liturgy*, Collegeville: Liturgical Press, 1986.

Huck, Gabriel and Chinchar, Gerald T., *Liturgy with Style and Grace*, Chicago: Liturgy Training Publications, 1984.

Hughes, Kathleen and Francis, Mary (eds), *Living No Longer for Ourselves: Liturgy and Justice in the Nineties*, Collegeville: Liturgical Press, 1991.

Hughes, Graham W., *Worship as Meaning: A Liturgical Theology for Late Modernity*, Cambridge: Cambridge University Press, 2003.

'Hymn to the Creator', in Vanstone, W. H., *Love's Endeavour, Love's Expense: The Response of Being to the Love of God*, London: Darton, Longman & Todd, 1977.

Iles, Paul, *The Pleasure of God's Company: A Handbook for Leading Intercessions*, Rattlesden: Kevin Mayhew, 1990.

Inge, John, *A Christian Theology of Place*, Farnham: Ashgate, 2003.

Instructions on Liturgical Formation in Seminaries, Rome: The Sacred Congregation for Catholic Education, 1979.

Irvine, Christopher, *The Cross and Creation in Christian Art and Liturgy*, London: SPCK, 2013.

James, Graham, 'Mission and the Parish-Shaped Church', *Theology*, 109:847, 2006.

Jenkins, Timothy, *An Experiment in Providence: How Faith Engages the World*, London: SPCK, 2006.

Jenkins, Timothy, 'An Approach to Anglican Formation', unpublished lecture given at Westcott House, Cambridge, 2007.

Kavanagh, Aidan OSB, *Elements of Rite: A Handbook of Liturgical Style*, Collegeville: Pueblo, 1982/90.

Kavanagh, Aidan OSB, *On Liturgical Theology*, Collegeville: Liturgical Press, 1992.

Laban, Rudolph, *The Mastery of Movement*, London: MacDonald & Evans, 1971.

Lampe, Peter, *From Paul to Valentinus: Christians at Rome in the First Two Centuries*, London: Continuum, 2003.

Langer, Suzanne, *Philosophy in a New Key: A Study in the Symbolism of Reason, Rite and Art*, Cambridge: Harvard University Press, 1942.

Larkin, Philip, *Collected Poems*, London: Faber & Faber, 2003.

Lawrence, D. H., 'Chaos in Poetry', in *Exchanges*, Iowa: University of Iowa, December 1929.

Learning Outcome Statement for Ordained Ministry in the Church of England, www.churchofengland.org/media/56877/The%20learning%20outcomes.doc.

Mayne, Michael, *Pray, Love, Remember*, London: Darton, Longman & Todd, 1998.

McGilchrist, Iain, *The Master and his Emissary: The Divided Brain and the Making of the Western World*, New Haven: Yale University Press, 2009.

McGowan, Andrew, 'Rethinking Eucharist Origins', *Pacifica* 23:2, 2010.

McVey, Kathleen E., 'The Domes of Church as Microcosm: Literary Roots of an Architectural Symbol', *Dumbarton Oaks Papers* 37, 1983, pp. 91–121.

Nida, Eugene A. and Tabor, Charles R., *The Theory and Practice of Translation*, Leiden: Brill, 1969.

Nielsen, Eduard, *Oral Tradition: A Modern Problem in the Old Testament Introduction*, London: SCM Press, 1954.

Nodet, Étienne and Taylor, Justin, *The Origins of Christianity: An Exploration*, Collegeville: Liturgical Press, 1998.

Papadopulos, Nicholas (ed.), *God's Transforming Work: Celebrating Ten Years of Common Worship*, London: SPCK, 2011.

Parker, T. H. L., *Calvin's Preaching*, Louisville: Westminster John Knox, 1992.

Percy, Martin, *Shaping the Church: The Promise of Implicit Theology*, Farnham: Ashgate, 2010.

Perham, Michael and Gray-Reeves, Mary, *The Hospitality of God*, London: SPCK, 2011.

Pickstock, Catherine, *After Writing: On the Liturgical Consummation of Philosophy*, Oxford: Blackwell, 1998.

Platten, Stephen and Lewis, Christopher (eds), *Dreaming Spires? Cathedrals in a New Age*, London: SPCK, 2006.

Putnam, Robert D. and Campbell, David E., *American Grace: How Religion Divides and Unites Us*, New York: Simon & Schuster, 2010.

Radcliffe, Timothy, *Jurassic Park and the Last Supper*, www.dominicans.ca/Documents/masters/Radcliffe/jurassic_park.html, 1996.

Ramshaw, Elaine, *Ritual and Pastoral Care*, Philadelphia: Fortress Press, 1987.

RCIA, Rite of Christian Initiation for Adults, www.liturgyoffice.org.uk/Resources/Rites/RCIA.pdf.

Robinson, Jonathan, *The Mass and Modernity: Walking to Heaven Backwards*, San Francisco: Ignatius Press, 2005.

Sadgrove, Michael, *Wisdom and Ministry: The Call to Leadership*, London: SPCK, 2008.

Sadgrove, Michael, *Landscapes of Faith: The Christian Heritage of the North East*, London: Third Millennium, 2013.

Saliers, Don E., *Worship as Theology: Foretaste of Glory Divine*, Nashville: Abingdon, 1994.

Schleiermacher, Friedrich, *On Religion: Speeches to its Cultural Despisers*, London: Trubner & Co., 1893.

Schwarz, Rudolph, *Vom Bau der Kirche*, Würzburg: Werkbundverlag, 1938; English edn: Harris, Cynthia, trans., *The Church Incarnate: The Sacred Function of Christian Architecture*, Chicago: Henry Regnery, 1958.

Sheldrake, Philip, *Spirituality and Theology: Christian Living and the Doctrine of God*, London: Darton, Longman & Todd, 1998.

Spence, Basil, *Phoenix at Coventry: The Building of a Cathedral*, London: Geoffrey Bles, 1962.

Spinks, Bryan D., 'Mis-shapen: Gregory Dix and the Four Action Shape of the Liturgy', *Lutheran Quarterly* 4, 1990, pp. 161–77.

Spinks, Bryan D., *The Sanctus in the Eucharistic Prayer*, Cambridge: Cambridge University Press, 1991.

Stancliffe, David, *God's Pattern: Shaping our Worship, Ministry and Life*, London: SPCK, 2003.

Stancliffe, David, *The Lion Companion to Church Architecture*, Oxford: Lion, 2008.

Stevenson, Kenneth W., *Jerusalem Revisited: The Liturgical Meaning of Holy Week*, Washington: Pastoral Press, 1988.

Stevenson, Kenneth W., *Wonderful and Sacred Mystery*, Washington: Pastoral Press, 1992.

Stringer, Martin, *Rethinking the Origins of the Eucharist*, London: SCM Press, 2011.

Taylor, John V., 'No Ordinary Place', unpublished talk to Guides at Winchester Cathedral, 1995.

Thomas, R. S., 'Introduction', in *The Oxford Book of Religious Verse*, Oxford: Oxford University Press, 1963.

Thomas, R. S., *Later Poems*, London: Macmillan, 1984.

Thomas, R. S., *Residues*, Tarset: Bloodaxe, 2002.

Torevell, David, *Losing the Sacred: Ritual, Modernity and Liturgical Reform*, Edinburgh: T&T Clark, 2000.

Tracey, David, *A Short History of the Interpretation of the Bible*, Augsburg: Fortress Press, 1988.

Vallés, Jules (trans. Parmee, Douglas), *The Child*, New York: New York Review of Books, 2004.

Vanstone, W. H., *Love's Endeavour, Love's Expense: The Response of Being to the Love of God*, London: Darton, Longman & Todd, 1977.

von Hügel, Friedrich, *Letter to a Niece*, Vancouver: Regent College Publishing, 2001.

Wainwright, Geoffrey, *Doxology: The Praise of God in Worship, Doctrine and Life: A Systematic Theology*, London: Epworth, 1980.

Wakefield, Gordon (ed.), *A Dictionary of Christian Spirituality*, London: SCM Press, 1983.

Walker, Andrew, *Telling the Story: Gospel, Mission and Culture*, London: SPCK, 1996.

Waugh, Evelyn, *Brideshead Revisited: The Sacred and Profane Memories of Captain Charles Ryder*, London: Chapman & Hall, 1948.

Wells, Samuel, *God's Companions: Reimagining Christian Ethics*, Oxford: Blackwell, 2006.

Wells, Samuel, 'The Power of Ministry', unpublished lecture to the Diocese of Wakefield Clergy Conference, 2012.

White, Susan J., *Christian Worship and Technological Change*, Nashville: Abingdon, 1994.

Williams, Rowan, *Lost Icons: Reflections on Cultural Bereavement*, Edinburgh: T&T Clark, 2000.

Willimon, William, *Worship as Pastoral Care*, Nashville: Abingdon, 1979.

Wright, N. T., *Jesus and the Victory of God*, London: SPCK, 1996.

Young, Frances M., *The Art of Performance: Towards a Theology of Holy Scripture*, London: Darton, Longman & Todd, 1990.

Index